MARY *in*
OUR CHRIST-LIFE

By WILLIAM JOSEPH CHAMINADE
MISSIONARY APOSTOLIC CANON OF BORDEAUX

Edited by BRO. WILLIAM J. KIEFER, S.M.
(MARIANIST)

THE BRUCE PUBLISHING COMPANY
MILWAUKEE

NIHIL OBSTAT:
    ROBERT BACKHERMS, S.M., S.T.D.
    Censor Deputatis

IMPRIMI POTEST:
    JAMES M. DARBY, S.M., Ph.D.
    Provincial

Feast of Holy Name of Mary
September 12, 1959

NIHIL OBSTAT:
    JOHN F. MURPHY, S.T.D.
    Censor librorum

IMPRIMATUR:
    ✠ WILLIAM E. COUSINS
    Archbishop of Milwaukee
    November 10, 1960

Preface

The following pages contain the jewels cut from the gem, i.e., the letters, essays, conferences, outlines and other writings of Father William Joseph Chaminade. It is said that a jeweler spends sometimes weeks and even months planning cuts he must make to get the very best jewels out of a gem. Similarly the author has spent several years reading and planning how he might cut these gems of Father Chaminade, so as to give the reader, for the time being, the heart jewel, if we may call it that. In fact the religious of the Society of Mary (Marianist), founded by Father Chaminade, have for nearly one hundred and fifty years been cutting those jewels for their own personal sanctification and the sanctification of their pupils.

In 1842, the world was astonished to find that such a work as the *True Devotion to Mary* of St. Louis Grignion de Montfort should be lost for so long. Catholics accepted the doctrine as a bright new star of devotion to Mary. In the not too distant future the world may be again astonished that the writings and doctrine of Father Chaminade, although hidden for even a longer time, hold for them a deep understanding of the age of Mary and the devotion to Mary called *Filial Piety* (love of a child for its mother). His genius stayed hidden in archives for so long mainly because there were not enough men of his genius and sanctity who could understand what he had to teach. Not too little blame can also be laid to the French Revolution and European upheaval of the past century.

To a vast majority of the laymen, and to many religious, Father Chaminade is a stranger. Although his own religious societies have been in America for over one hundred years, yet they have for humble reasons failed to share sufficiently with others their founder's doctrines on Mariology and asceticism. But at last there is promise of bringing to the world the writings of a man who spiritually directed and organized what we now call Catholic

Action more than one hundred and fifty years ago. Even more impetus is added as the cause for beatification is being studied in the Roman court.

Father Chaminade was a man of action in the fullest sense of the word. He published no books, although he wrote dozens of pages of letters, notes, and articles every day of his priestly life. His driving conviction was to multiply and increase apostles among the laity so fast that the world would be revitalized in a short time. He planned to use men and women of every age and of every degree of spirituality and of every type of occupation to prove by example to the rationalistic and materialistic world that Christianity was not an antiquated institution, and that the Gospel of Christ was still as practicable today as it was nearly two thousand years ago.

He stressed that his time was the beginning of the age of Mary and, as she conquered every other heresy, she would appear and conquer this worst of evils, religious indifference and the enormous apostasy from the faith of Christ. Father Chaminade proclaimed the prerogative of Mary's Immaculate Conception some fifty years before its dogmatic proclamation by Pope Pius IX. Many of the things we speak of commonly about the Blessed Virgin and the participation of the laity in the work of the clergy, Father Chaminade spoke of clearly and boldly in his day while others felt safe in only intimating their beliefs. Not only was he convinced of the importance of these doctrines, but moreover he organized the laity under Mary's Immaculate Conception to accomplish this gigantic task of spiritual renovation. In 1869, almost twenty years after the death of Father Chaminade, Cardinal Donnet of Bordeaux spoke in astonishment of what he found accomplished by Father Chaminade. This declaration is even more interesting when we learn that the Cardinal several times had misunderstandings with the saintly founder and his religious societies. To the Marianists, the Cardinal wrote, "Father Chaminade was a saint and an eminent and respectable man. We do not properly know him or appreciate him; we hardly remember him as we ought. Yet should you trace any apostolic work in Bordeaux to its origin after the French Revolution, you will find at the beginning of every one of them the name of Father Chaminade."

Father Gabriel M. Roschini, O.S.M., a great Italian Mariologist of our day, places Father William Chaminade among the best Mariologists of the past century. Among the religious leaders of France, Father Chaminade ranks with St. Vincent de Paul, St. John Bosco, and St. Philip Neri for his work in education. Father Chaminade hoped by Catholic Action and education to stem the tide of modern rationalism and secularism that turned the eighteenth and nineteenth centuries into an intellectual and spiritual nightmare. Spiritual writers and theologians accept Father Chaminade into their ranks because of his deep understanding of asceticism and mysticism. He was always working to mix "Martha" and "Mary" in the right proportions so as to obtain a perfect saint and apostle for modern times.

Quickly, the reader will discover that the pages of this book are not those of the common spiritual reading book. Father Chaminade never wrote books for spiritual reading. All his life he winnowed the chaff from the wheat and what he gave his spiritual sons and daughters were the purest and deepest meditational considerations of God and the Blessed Virgin. His long hours of reading and writing were similar to the long ages it takes to form a gem. But Father Chaminade was not merely satisfied to pass on to the ages a gem merely dug from the earth. No, he wanted us to receive a polished gem with all the foreign matter cut away. Jewels are meant to look at from every possible angle, since brilliant light comes from every angle. And when you feel that you have seen every possible fraction of light, go back and look again. You will be sure to find another light from heaven that you missed before. As there is no end to the new vistas of spiritual life in reading and meditating on the Gospel, or the *Imitation of Christ*, so there will be no end to reading the heart of Father William Joseph Chaminade.

W. J. K.

Acknowledgments

This compilation of quotations could not be accomplished without the tireless and exacting research of many people whose findings and translations were used. In particular there are four doctors of Sacred Theology to whom we owe much of the writing of this little book. We are most grateful to Norbert C. Burns, S.M., S.T.D.; William J. Cole, S.M., S.T.D.; John Harrington, S.M., S.T.D.; and Thomas A. Stanley, S.M., S.T.D. They wrote scholarly theses; they did most of the research in old musty archives; they made most of the translations.

The author of this book like a gardener went through the flower beds and culled out those flowers he thought would best fit into a beautiful bouquet to edify us poor sinners, to honor Father William Joseph Chaminade, to give homage to the Blessed Virgin Mary, and glorify God, the Creator of heaven and earth.

Also our gratitude is extended to the eminent Mariologist, Father Emil Neubert, S.M., Father Theodore Koehler, S.M., and to the Very Reverend Good Father Paul Joseph Hoffer, S.M., Superior General of the Society of Mary, for their encouragement and generous suggestions in the preparation of this book.

Introduction

As the eighteenth century was nearing its close, after the French
Revolution that had overturned all France, Divine Providence, that
ever most admirably rules and guides individuals and peoples, raised
up in the bosom of Holy Church a group of men and priests endowed with knowledge, virtue, and piety, and destined to repair
the general ruin, to restore Christian faith and morals, and to re-
establish peace and order.

Among these we reckon the faithful servant of God, William
Joseph Chaminade, a priest who founded the Society of Mary. As
a valiant missionary he went about southwestern France, especially
in the diocese of Bordeaux and neighboring dioceses, and spent
himself in religious works and preaching.

He was born April 8, 1761, at Perigueux, the thirteenth child
of devout and respected parents. The same day he was baptized
and given the name of William. At home he received a truly
Christian training. He used to accompany his mother to church
and pray fervently during the services. At the age of ten he was
confirmed. On this occasion he added the name Joseph to his
baptismal name because of the special devotion and confidence he
felt toward the Virgin Mother of God and her chaste spouse. He
received his elementary instruction in his native city, and then in
the neighboring town of Mussidan diligently studied the humanities.
Two of his brothers, one a priest, were in charge of the college.
There, while he was entirely occupied with his studies and devotions, he made his First Communion, much to his own joy and

the edification of those who were present. Because of his outstanding merit he was even admitted while yet a student to the Congregation of St. Charles, which consisted of the professors of the college. He was, furthermore, so eminent in virtue that his spiritual guides easily allowed him to make private religious vows.

About this time he severely injured his foot. When after two months of treatment he saw that no medical remedy would help, he put his confidence in the Mother of God and promised to make a pilgrimage to her much frequented shrine at Verdelais. His foot healed remarkably fast, so that he was soon able to undertake on foot that rather long journey and to carry out the pilgrimage he had promised.

He studied his philosophy at Bordeaux and began his theology there. He finished it in Paris at the Seminary of St. Sulpice, and won special praise for his application and progress in study. He obtained a degree in theology and was then advanced to the priest-hood at the age of twenty-four.

Returning to Mussidan, to his two brothers, John Baptist and Louis, now a priest as they were, he lent them valuable assistance by his devotedness as professor and treasurer. Their united efforts restored to the college, which was somewhat on the decline, its former renown and prosperity. At the same time Joseph exercised his sacred ministry with much fruit at the hospital and in the churches, especially at the shrine of the Blessed Virgin called Notre Dame du Roc, to which he zealously strove to increase and propagate devotion among the faithful.

With the rise in 1789 of that storm against Church and State in France that overturned political and religious institutions, Joseph and his brothers refused with manly steadfastness and Christian intrepidity to take the oath required of ecclesiastics by the Civil Constitution of the Clergy.

Then it was that the servant of God left the college of Mussidan and toward the close of 1791 took up his abode in Bordeaux. There he was impelled to remain in hiding. Admirably uniting prudence and zeal, he went about unharmed — thanks to the protection of the Mother of God — to homes and hiding places and administered the consolations of religion to the healthy and the infirm. He also strove to bring unfaithful priests back to the fold. He received their acts of abjuration in an oratory he had set up for the faithful, and then labored to keep them loyal to their faith.

Soon a severe decree was issued exiling all priests who were resolved to obey God rather than man. Joseph, therefore, went to Spain in 1797 and took refuge at Saragossa. Here for three years he lived by the labor of his hands in making plaster statues. His leisure moments he employed in studying questions of monastic life and asceticism and in doing works of charity. But above all he prayed often and devoutly at the shrine of Our Lady of the Pillar. In later years, Joseph himself declared that before that famous altar he had first been enlightened from on high and inspired to found the Society of Mary.

As soon as circumstances allowed, he returned to his residence at Bordeaux, where with much zeal and labor he directed and developed various societies of young men and young women, of fathers and mothers, of workmen and of professional men, all united in a vast Sodality of the Immaculate Conception. The center of this Sodality and its works he established at the Chapel of St. Mary Magdalene. Authorized witnesses and the records of the tribunal of inquiry for the Cause clearly reveal how much excellent fruit came forth from this Sodality with its affiliates in the city and archdiocese of Bordeaux and in other dioceses, especially in the neighboring one of Bazas, administered by the servant of God for a while and later incorporated into the archdiocese.

Moreover, upon the suggestion of Joseph Chaminade, and under his guidance, a pious lady, Marie Theresa de Lamourous, established at Bordeaux an institution known as the Misericorde where girls that had become victims of passion and were on the way to perdition could find a well-equipped refuge from dangerous worldly contacts and allurements, and enter upon a new life of virtue and piety.

Finally the hour was at hand when with the help of God he could put into execution the design which by inspiration from on high he had conceived at Saragossa before the shrine of our Lady. As a prelude to this undertaking he formed a band of fifteen sodalists who engaged themselves to live as religious in the world and to devote themselves completely to action of spiritual mercy toward their brethren. At length in 1817 the servant of God and several chosen souls offered and consecrated themselves to God at the altar under the auspices of Mary and thus laid the foundation of the Society of Mary. From that day to this present time, this Institute comprising the three classes of priests, lay members engaged in teaching, and artisans has more and more increased its numbers and extended its action. On September 5, 1818, with the approbation of the Archbishop, these first members pronounced the three ordinary vows of religion, to which they added those of stability and of forming and multiplying true Christians and good citizens by teaching.

Another spiritual family called the Daughters of Mary had also been organized by Father Chaminade. The superioress, Miss Adelaide de Trenquelleon, and her first religious made their profession in the hands of the Founder himself. Under his direction two Third Orders of the Daughters of Mary were added, one of seculars and one of regulars. The latter, although not bound to enclosure, nevertheless, kept the observances of their Institute very faithfully and engaged in pious works principally in country districts.

Having completed this series of foundations, the servant of God, octogenarian though he was and rich in merit, was subject by permission of Heaven to a most painful trial. By having thus to walk the royal way of the Cross in hardship and opposition, he strengthened his already eminent virtue and rendered it only more evident.

The servant of God had now reached the decline of his life. Wasted in body by labor and broken in spirit by care, on January 6, 1850, while listening to some spiritual reading, he was suddenly stricken with apoplexy. His members were paralyzed and he lost his power of speech but retained the full use of his mental faculties. The pastor of St. Aloysius Church in Bordeaux administered Holy Viaticum and Extreme Unction to him. On the twenty-second of that same January, after having imparted his paternal blessing to his children gathered around his bedside, he kissed his crucifix and in the act of pressing it to his heart rendered his soul to God. The funeral took place amid a great concourse of the clergy and laity. His mortal remains were interred in the cemetery of the Chartreuse, where they now rest in peace.

His portrait has been carved on the monument erected over his remains, and an epitaph recalls his memory and renders honor to his works.

The fame of the sanctity of the servant of God which manifested itself during his life as well as after his death grew steadily. This it was that induced the ordinaries of Bordeaux and Vitoria to undertake the process of information known as *de fama sanctitatis*. (Here is then stated the various steps taken and the Church authorities identified who were responsible for bringing the case before Congregation of Rites in Rome.) Finally, all sides of the question and case having been carefully pondered, their Eminences the Cardinals of the Congregation of Rites, agreed to reply: "The Commission for the Introduction of the Cause may be introduced, if it please His Holiness (Pope Benedict XV)." This was May the seventh, 1918.

A report of all these proceedings having been delivered by the undersigned Cardinal, Pro-Prefect of the Congregation of Rites, to our Most Holy Father Pope Benedict XV, His Holiness, ratifying the response of the Sacred Congregation, deigned to sign *Propria manu* the Commission for the Introduction of the Cause of the Servant of God, William Joseph Chaminade, priest and founder of the Society of Mary, on the eighth day of May, 1918.

A. Cardinal Vico
Bishop of Porto and Santa Rufina,
Pro-Prefect of the Holy Congregation of Rites.

Contents

PART ONE Mary, Mother of God and Our Mother

I. Knowledge of Mary. II. Greatness of Mary. III. Divine Maternity of Mary. IV. Mary Is Our Mother. V. Mary at the Cross on Calvary. VI. Mary, Our Queen and Mediatrix.

I. In What It Consists. II. Love of Mary Our Mother. III. Union of Jesus and Mary. IV. Missionaries of Mary.

I. The Head and the Members. II. The Spirit of Christ in the Mystical Body. III. Sacraments of the Mystical Body.

PART TWO *Perfection and the Means to Attain It*

PART ONE

Mary, Mother of God and Our Mother

> I am thoroughly convinced that our Savior has reserved to His Blessed Mother the glory of being the main support of the Holy Church in these latter times.
>
> — Fr. Chaminade to Pope Gregory XVI, September 16, 1838

CHAPTER ONE

Mary, Mother of All Mankind

I. KNOWLEDGE OF MARY

Knowledge precedes appreciation and appreciation precedes conviction. After conviction comes love and action — life's goal. That being true, Father Chaminade earnestly tells us that we must know and study Mary in the divine economy of our salvation, if we are to appreciate and to love Mary as the Mother of Christ and the Mother of every baptized soul.

This is Mary, the Mother of God! In her presence let every knee bend in heaven, on earth, and under the earth. Oh, the depth of the riches of God we may exclaim with the great Apostle. The Eternal Word deigns to be born of a woman, to owe her His life, and, by the fact, honor and obedience; the creature conceives her Creator. Jesus, owing His body solely to her body from which alone the Holy Spirit has formed it, she concentrates upon her Son the rights and the duties of both a father and a mother.

Mary, the Mother of God! Heaven is in her chaste womb; the Divinity resides there bodily, veiled, it is true, but not destroyed, under the form of a slave. And, when Jesus shall have seen the light of day, He will be admired as depending on and subject to Mary, as would be an ordinary child, conceived in the pain of sin. The Son of God will permit Himself to be nursed, clad, fed, and educated by a creature that fulfills toward Him all the duties of a mother. Apparently powerless to sustain Himself and to provide for His needs, the Word Eternal, as a helpless babe, will rest upon the knee of Mary, and, close to her heart, He will be nourished with milk from her breast. He will invite her tender cares, keep near her feet, and listen with all docility.

Mary, the Mother of God, in a certain way is also His teacher! Hers is the honor, not only to give the Son of God life and His physical education, but at the same time she has the glory of giving Him His moral education. God, her Son, must in the eyes of men, grow in wisdom and age; not that He is ignorant of anything, or needs to learn anything, since in Him are all the treasures of wisdom and of knowledge; but, having annihilated Himself under the form of a human person, He assumed exteriorly, in passing through the various stages of life, all that was not sin; all, I say, even, during His infancy, the appearance of ignorance and feebleness. Thus it was that angels and men could contemplate the Creator in the school of a creature that knows nothing except through Him.

Mary the Mother of God, unto the end, will have subject to her the Word Eternal made flesh in her virginal womb. Jesus will be subject to her unto death, unto the death on the cross. His Mother will be consulted in all things unless the Heavenly Father should ordain otherwise. He will even submit to her consent the very operations of the Holy Spirit in her soul, that He might teach us how to subdue our pride in vain knowledge to the authority and spiritual direction of those whom the Lord hath placed over us, whoever they may be.

Finally, Mary, the Mother of God, a surpassing and incomprehensible mystery, entitling a feeble creature to call God her Son, and to share not with mortal spouse, but with the Eternal Father Himself, if I may say so, the rights to the homage and the filial devotedness of Jesus Christ! Such is the teaching of the Holy Church. She calls her Mary, the Mother of Jesus. Let us, therefore, learn the Mother through the Son.

Moreover, this study of Mary is interesting and sublime of its own nature and of prime importance for our welfare. Mary, the Mother of God! Mary, the New Eve, and, as such, co-operating with the New Adam at the regeneration of men. Consequently, too, the Mother of Christians, fulfilling the mother's duty in their regard! Mary our Mediatrix with her divine Son! Finally, Mary raised because of her virtues to the sublimest heights a creature is capable of! Such are her prerogatives that we must ponder over and admire.

Did we but know her, did we but understand her tender solicitude for the children whom God confided to her care, could we but divine all the tender ingenuity of her loving heart to avert the universal deluge menacing the faith and the morals of humankind, we should be far more devoted to her. Her name would more frequently and more hopefully pass our lips, and with keener delight would we partake of her sweet bounty.

Daily we speak of Mary, we flock to her altars; we glory in being her children; yet whatever we do know of her is but a trifle, a faint idea of what she is in reality regarding God and ourselves, in the order of faith. How many Christians could not our Blessed Lady reproach in the terms that our Savior addressed to His people by the mouth of Isaias the Prophet: "The ox knoweth his owner, and the ass his master's crib; but Israel hath not known me, and my people hath not understood" (Isa. 1:3). Not to merit such a shameful reproach, let us study all we can concerning our Mother and Queen. We must know her.

You will infallibly get to know and relish the virtues of our Lord Jesus Christ, the true model of Christians and religious, if you will remember this bit of wisdom. Indeed, the Blessed Virgin is our model, too, but just because she is a very exact and perfect copy of Jesus Christ, her adorable Son. It is the knowledge of our Lord Jesus Christ which leads us to the knowledge of the Blessed Virgin, as truly as the knowledge of the Blessed Virgin leads us to a higher degree of knowledge of our Lord Jesus Christ.

We all know that the knowledge of Jesus Christ is indispensable for our salvation, for, as "sole Mediator between God and Man," He only "has the words of eternal life," and our "sufficiency is from God" (1 Tim. 2:5; 2 Cor. 3:5; Jn. 6:9). Finally, only He can and does save us. But not underrating in any way this fundamental belief, we furthermore hold that the knowledge of Mary contributes largely toward our salvation, because, as St. Bernard tells us, "Mary is the cause of our hope."

II. GREATNESS OF MARY

Mary has the greatest and clearest claims to our homage and praise. She is the Mother of a mortal king, but more than that she is the Mother of the Prince of the eternal empire. She is the Mother of mankind, the Coredemptrix of men, the Salvation of the world. She is a descendant of David whose royal blood flows in her veins. Yet this title to Mary's greatness is eclipsed by her supreme dignity of Mother of God and her other prerogatives. The august Virgin is the height of perfection among the works of the Creator.

Of Mary we may assert the same as the Apostle does of heaven: "Eye hath not seen, ear hath not heard, nor hath it entered into the heart of man" to conceive the transcending excellence of the august Mother of God. The mystery of a woman's elevation to the signal honor of conceiving in her womb and giving birth to a God; the mystery of a virgin becoming a mother without ceasing to be a virgin; lastly, the mystery of a creature possessing and exercising a father's and mother's rights over God as her Son, behold here is the sublime spectacle of the Divine Maternity.

To accomplish the great mystery of God made man, it was providential to have the concurrence of a woman who, by her virtue and her purity, would live according to the great prerogative of the Divine Maternity. It was fitting to confer upon a human being the untold privilege of giving life, in time, to the very Son of the Most High. Mary was that great desired one. In consequence of her Fiat she will become the privileged Daughter of the Father, the Mother of the Son, and the Spouse of the Holy Spirit, united to the Holy Trinity by a triple alliance, giving rise to the sweet appellations of daughter, mother, and spouse. As such, the perfection of her being will correspond to her incomprehensible exaltation, for the Mother of God must be endowed by God, her Son, with every attribute becoming her surpassing dignity.

Consequently the human tongue cannot express in words the excellence of Mary as Mother of God. By applying to her St. Paul's description of heaven we still fall short of reality. Heaven is but the temple of God, while Mary is His maternal sanctuary. Heaven but contains God and, even at that, does not suffice to contain Him as Holy Church tells us; whereas Mary conceived and bore Him in her womb.

Mary's rank is that of Mother of God. If there is no one above the Mother of God but God Himself, the veneration we render to Mary must so far surpass every other veneration as the dignity of Mother of God surpasses all others; it is inferior only to God alone.

Our dependence upon Mary is complete. If we could be independent of her in some matter, her maternal solicitude in this particular matter would be nullified. This very idea would be repugnant to the works of love, gratitude, and obedience which her divine Son had operated in her. This complete dependence, besides demonstrating, as her Divine Maternity does, our duty of rendering her a very special veneration, furthermore proves that at all times and in all places we should pray to Mary and honor her.

Oh, the blindness and illusion of Christians who give to Mary what does not belong to her. When calling Mary *Spes nostra* — our Hope — let us remember that it is through Jesus that she is our hope. When invoking her as *Refugium peccatorum* — the Refuge of sinners — let us remember her as protectress only of those willing to give up their sins, not of those loving them. She is the *Mater misericordiae* — Mother of mercies — because she has given to the world Him who is all-merciful.

We are accused of pompously eulogizing Mary and are criticized for the honor we render her. I do not refer only to the impious but to the badly instructed Christians who know not the gift of God in this miracle of His omnipotence. Can we really assert too much, do too much, provided we do not declare her equal to the Divinity, provided we make a distinction between her veneration and that of the Divinity? What hath God said of Mary? What hath He done for her? Surely, He is our Model.

It is in the designs of Divine Wisdom that we should unceasingly discover new beauties in the most excellent work He accomplished by forming the Blessed Virgin. God always casts out new lights from the treasures of His goodness and mercy in order to make us admire Mary, in order to excite our confidence in her.

III. DIVINE MATERNITY OF MARY

If we wish to speak of a fundamental principle of Mariology, the dogma of the Divine Maternity — that Mary is Mother of the God-Man — is that principle, recognized by many scholars. From this point Father Chaminade begins all his thoughts on the Blessed Virgin. But he never considered Mary the Mother of God alone; it is always in relation to the salvation of mankind and the spiritual maternity of the Mystical Body of Christ. Hence, we may be more correct to say that the fundamental principle of Mariology for Father Chaminade is that of the Divine-Spiritual Maternity.

The mystery of a woman raised to the exalted dignity of Mother of her God; the mystery of a virgin becoming a mother without ceasing to be a virgin; the mystery of a creature possessing and exercising at the same time the rights of a parent over God who is her Son — this is the astounding mystery of Mary's Divine Maternity.

As marked children of guilty parents, we, too, would have been engulfed in their ruin. But moved with compassion for the masterpiece of His hands, God conceived the ineffable design of restoring the human race from the state of degradation into which it had fallen, and of reconciling earth with heaven. In order to satisfy the infinite justice of God, to confound the powers of hell, and to show forth more and more the glory of His heavenly Father, the Son of God offered Himself to take the place of guilty man.

In a word, He, the Son of God, offered to become man like us and to take our iniquities upon Himself in order to expiate them by shedding His sacred blood. He would unite Himself to us and thus make us divine in Him, so that being one with Him, we might once more and with even greater truth than ever before call God our Father. He, therefore, offered Himself as a victim, and His sacrifice being accepted, our redemption was decided upon in the august council of the Most Holy Trinity. This was the consoling revelation made to our first parents after their fall, in the very place of their crime, so that the hope of a Savior in time to come might mitigate the appalling evils consequent upon their sin.

The promised Redeemer had to be man, so that He might merit and suffer; He had likewise to be God, so that His merits might possess the infinite value that alone could strictly satisfy the justice of the Most High. To this end He must have two natures entirely distinct, His humanity and His divinity, which, being united in Him by an admirable bond without confusion and admixture, should constitute only a single person. If, by the sublimity of His eternal nature, He is one with God the Father, He was to become by the infirmity of His mortal nature like unto us and one of us. As He chose to take upon Himself human nature, He wished, like other men, to be born, to suffer, and to die. A woman was therefore to conceive and bear Him in her womb, bring Him forth to human life, nourish Him at her breast, teach Him to speak, support Him when He was still weak; and this privileged woman was to be the Mother of God.

Mary was to take an active part in communicating this supernatural life to man. That is implied in the words of God Himself when, in the hearing of our first parents, and on the very scene of their crime, He addressed the serpent in these words, "I shall create enmity between thee and the woman, between her seed and thy seed, and she shall crush thy head." Mary is the woman referred to, who was to co-operate in the destruction of the empire of Satan, which is death, and in the establishment of the kingdom of justice, which is life upon earth. Mary, the New Eve, was therefore to concur effectively in the regeneration of the human race.

Mary was thus prepared and chosen, and was, therefore, in view of her incomparable dignity, the object of the predilection of the Most Holy Trinity even before her creation. It pleased God to sketch in broad outlines her magnificent features, now under one figure, now under another, make her known in advance to the world whose hope and glory she was some day to be.

Jesus Christ, our divine Savior, seems to have taken it upon Himself to show, by His manner of addressing His Blessed Mother, that she is in truth the New Eve. In the first place, He was pleased, during His mortal life, to call her by the great name of Woman. This fact is remarkable, for there can be no doubt that in regard to Mary, His Mother, Jesus was the most tender, the most loving, and the most respectful of sons. If however, He always addressed her as Woman, even in that most sublime moment of His life when He was about to consummate the sacrifice of redemption on the altar of the cross, He must have considered it the most august and the most appropriate name, the name that would express in its truest sense her position in regard to humanity and to Himself.

Though we do not pretend to reject the various interpretations by which some have sought to justify the seeming inconsiderateness on the part of the Son of God in this particular point, yet may we not say that the paramount reason why the Savior of mankind should make use of the name "Woman" when speaking to His Mother was precisely to make us understand and to remind us unceasingly of the one great fact that she is indeed the New Eve, promised in the very words that announced the Redeemer of the world?

At length the fullness of time had arrived, and behold, Mary came overflowing with delights and radiant with beauty. All the foreshadowing figures of the Old Law now fade into insignificance before the sublime reality. Only too long mankind had toiled on amid the most fatal experiences of its own weakness and misery; only too long patriarchs and prophets had sighed for the Lord. Now at last the clouds shall rain down the Just One, and the earth shall bring forth the Savior.

At Nazareth, under the protection of a husband, there lived a humble Virgin of the royal family of David, unknown to man, but beloved by God. Her dwelling was as unpretentious as her person. Joseph supported her by the labor of his hands. All her beauty was from within, and it was perfect beauty, free from every blemish and shadow. While tired nature was resting, while all that breathed and had life under heaven was wrapped in slumber, Mary was at prayer in the silence of her home. Her heart beat fast, her soul was all aflame, in transport she called to the help of man Him who was to come.

Little did she know then that she was the one who was chosen to give birth to the Son of the Eternal One. She was, therefore, startled at the sight of the celestial messenger, gracious in the form of a young man, bright and beautiful. Yet the penetrating gaze of the Virgin recognized the heavenly visitor, and filled with the sentiment of her personal unworthiness, she was first surprised, then visibly troubled at such a messenger. Her fear went so far that the heavenly envoy had to reassure her before disclosing the sublime object of his mission. He then went on to tell her about the mystery of the Incarnation, and the choice that God had made of her to be the Mother of His Son. Mary, being reassured by the explanation of the angel, resigned herself to the signal honor of the Divine Maternity, and submitted in all simplicity to the unspeakable operation of the Holy Spirit within her. At that moment the Word was made flesh, humbled, in her chaste womb, under the form of a slave.

Then the faith of Mary was entire and more perfect than that of Abraham which earned for him the title and quality of Father of believers. The faith of the prophets, the Apostles, and the entire Church cannot approach hers. Relying on the word of God, she believed something which will always be the despair of feeble reason, and she believed so firmly that by the force of her faith, hoping against all hope, she became the Mother of God and men.

The Spirit of God who miraculously formed the body of Jesus Christ in Mary's virginal womb from her most pure blood also formed the soul of Mary after that of Jesus Christ. He impressed upon her all the characteristics of His resemblance in such a way that just as, according to nature, Jesus Christ received the life of Mary, in the same way in the order of grace Mary received the life of her adorable Son and became entirely like Him. The characteristics of conformity were of the greatest perfection because Mary corresponded with a complete and perfect fidelity.

Finally in Scripture we read, "Mary, the Virgin of whom was born Jesus." Here we perceived the acme of her glory. Hence this mystery is the cause of our veneration for her and the motive of our confidence in her. This is the principle and likewise the doctrine regulating our devotion to the Blessed Virgin. Also it is our caution against two snares. The one being to confine our worship of Mary too narrowly, thus destroying the firm foundation of our confidence and depriving us of a most powerful means of salvation.

The other, giving overmuch attention to exterior practices, being more zealous in honoring her virtues than in imitating them, and under the pretext of piety to condone our failings and impenitence.

IV. MARY IS OUR MOTHER

A prominent Flemish theologian a few years ago quoted a whole page of passages from Father Chaminade on the Spiritual Maternity of Mary for a Mariological periodical, Marianum. His conclusion was thus: "We could not select any texts more beautiful than those of Father William Chaminade to gather, in one page the origin and development of the Catholic doctrine which teaches that Mary is our Mother." (G. Geenen, O.P., Marie Notre Mere, Marianum, Vol. 10, 1948, pp. 351–352.)

Before Father Chaminade the Spiritual Maternity of Mary was almost entirely neglected or if it was mentioned, the only basis given for it was the donation of our Lord to St. John, as He was about to expire on the cross. It was under these conditions that Father Chaminade developed a remarkable doctrine of the Spiritual Maternity, which would mark him as a precursor of modern thought on the subject.

Father Chaminade's insistence on the Spiritual Maternity of Mary, which is the basis of a sonlike devotion to her, results from two factors: (1) the needs of the times, in which any idea of slavery and inferiority would be repugnant, and (2) the intimate conviction of Father Chaminade that our relation to Mary must be a reproduction of that which existed between Christ and His Mother. Because of our oneness with Christ in the Mystical Body, we are not simply slaves and servants of Mary, but really one Son of Mary with Jesus Christ.[1]

The idea that Mary became our Mother spiritually at the moment that she conceived the Son of God seems to be the first of several doctrines that are original with Father Chaminade. There are faint indications of it in the French school of spirituality, but nowhere is the doctrine so definitely stated as by him. Only in

---

[1] Thesis of Rev. William J. Cole, S.M., S.T.D., "The Spiritual Maternity of Mary according to Fr. W. J. Chaminade," pp. iii–iv.

recent times has this idea been developed in the principal of maternal grace of Mary.

One point further. The reader may ask which in this book is the doctrine of the Spiritual Maternity of Mary. The answer is that the whole book is a development of the doctrine. Father Chaminade never separated theory from practice any more than he separated the Divine Maternity from the Spiritual Maternity or attempted to separate spirituality into departments. There is no Mary without Jesus, no Mystical Body without Jesus, no Incarnation without Redemption, and there is no knowledge of these things without the totality of existence in these things. Thus the arrangements of the sections of this book are arbitrary.

Here is the first fundamental consideration of the Motherhood of Mary: Christ "who was conceived of the Holy Ghost, born of the Virgin Mary." It was in the womb of our Blessed Lady that Jesus Christ was conceived of the Holy Spirit and took up our nature save sin; in this virginal womb of Mary also the elect must be conceived by the operation of the Holy Spirit and formed according to the image of Jesus Christ by her maternal care.

The Blessed Virgin Mary is not our Mother solely because she had adopted us as her children, as is commonly believed, but she is our Mother really and truly because she has given us spiritual birth just as she really gave birth to Jesus Christ.

The Blessed Virgin is called not only the Mother of Jesus, but also the Mother of the elect and of all the children of God, because (a) she has brought them forth unto supernatural life; (b) she has exercised maternal care over them; (c) she has shown them her tender love and affection.

"No one can lay another foundation, but that which is already laid, which is Christ Jesus," says St. Paul (1 Cor. 3:11). It is upon Jesus Christ also that we undertake to lay the foundation of our devotion to the Blessed Virgin. It is an immovable foundation which the enemies of our faith seek in vain to undermine. Jesus Christ, today, yesterday, and forever; hence our devotion to Mary will be eternal.

How is the Blessed Virgin our true Mother?
We all have life in Christ;
Christ took life in the womb of Mary;
We are one with Christ in His Mystical Body;

Therefore, we also took spiritual life in Mary.

It is for this reason that the Fathers say that Mary is the book of the generation of Jesus Christ and of all beings. It is in her that they are all included.

This book of the generation of Jesus Christ, which closes with these words: Mary of whom Jesus was born, is the book of all those who are incorporated in Jesus Christ, or those who become His coheirs. It is the book of life in which are inscribed the names of the predestined.

Ah, rejoice, our Lord Jesus Christ tells us, that your names are written in the book of life. Behold her who engendered you spiritually to the Faith when she conceived me corporally in her virginal womb; she is your Mother just as she is mine, undoubtedly not by the same title, but nevertheless by a title of spiritual generation. What is this book of life except Mary in her generation?

Mary is really our Mother in the order of grace; she has given us our being of grace. Since we are accustomed to judge things only by our senses, we are almost always aware only of our natural life. But how much more excellent is our supernatural life? How long will our natural life exist? Our supernatural life is destined to be eternal. Our natural life ends with death and the tomb. Our supernatural life will be a blessed and eternal life.

We must not imagine, according to the remark of the great Bossuet that the Blessed Virgin is but a simple canal by which all graces and the author of them come to us. We owe to the Blessed Virgin the ineffable mystery of the Incarnation and by it our Head of the Mystical Body. Mary is the source of that plenitude in order to transmit it to us *maternally*. It is in this sense that the angel salutes her as full of grace, and that pious scholars apply to her the text of St. John: "of his fullness we have all received."

But by what operation did Mary conceive us? It was by the operation of the Holy Spirit. It was in her supereminent being of grace that the Virgin Mary conceived us. It was in the ardor of her charity that she communicated to us her being of grace, which is but a participation in that of Christ.

Mary by the mystery of the Incarnation had become Mother of Mercy Itself, Mother of Charity, and one should not fear to say that it is by the ardor of her charity that she conceived the Son of God spiritually at the same time that she conceived Him naturally. In becoming Mother of the Savior of the world and her Savior, she becomes Mother of Christians. Judge from this the extent of her love.

It is this grace of the Incarnation which makes Christians the children of God, the brothers of Jesus Christ, and the heirs of heaven. Consequently, there is neither on earth nor in heaven any justified soul, anyone of the elect, who does not owe to Mary his justice and his glory. God, as it were, had subordinated the execution of the mystery of the incarnation to the will, to the charity of Mary. Therefore, all must respect the charity of this incomparable Virgin.

How happy are the true children of Mary! The Mother of Jesus truly becomes their Mother. Perhaps you will say that Mary cannot be your Mother as she is the Mother of Jesus. Without doubt, if we do not consider things according to the spirit; but it is particularly according to the spirit that we ought to envisage the Divine Maternity rather than according to nature. Mary, according to the words of Jesus Christ Himself, was happier to have given Him birth spiritually than according to the order of nature (cf. Lk. 11:27–28).

From what precedes we must conclude that Mary is our Mother not merely by adoption, but also, and above all, by spiritual regeneration. It follows likewise that she became our Mother when she conceived the Son of God. The Incarnation therefore, considered in its necessary result, is the fruit of the divine espousal of the Holy Ghost and the august Virgin. It is a spiritual yet fruitful espousal that gave life in the natural order to her Son, Jesus Christ, and produced, in the spiritual order, that is, by faith, the regeneration of mankind.

We do not belong to Mary merely from the time that our Savior confided us to her love. On Mount Calvary, it is true, the price of our redemption was paid to divine justice. That was the consummation of our redemption. On the cross, Jesus merited for us the grace of adoption and of glory. On Mount Calvary, Mary in whose bosom we were spiritually conceived since the Incarnation, brought us forth to the life of faith. But it was not only then that she became our Mother; for, if we were her children only since Calvary, the words of our divine Savior, "Woman, behold thy son," would in a more or less restricted sense have indeed made us her adopted children. Jesus would indeed be the only one born if we were merely adopted children, for adopted children are not children by birth. How then could the Blessed Virgin, strictly speaking, fulfill the functions of the New Eve in our regard? Besides, the relation established between the Blessed Virgin and ourselves by mere adoption would not suffice to satisfy all our needs. We must have a mother, a true and real mother, in the order of faith as in the order of nature. In the one as in the other an adopted mother cannot replace a real mother.

By those remarkable words, "Woman, behold thy son," Jesus dying on the cross revealed to the world a truth that is most important for our salvation. He reserved this revelation for the supreme moment of His life, to give it all the sacredness of the last will and testament of God. And may we not be justified in saying that it was the divine intention not to reveal the maternity of Mary until the day when she, at the foot of the cross, should show herself our Mother by sacrificing, for our salvation, the God-man.

This, it seems to us, is the meaning and the purport of the beautiful words of Jesus. In saying to the beloved disciple, "Behold thy Mother," He wished to say thereby, "Behold her who bore you spiritually to the faith when she conceived Me corporally in her virginal womb. She is your Mother as she is Mine, not indeed in the same manner but by the right of generation." Thus also by these words addressed to Mary, "Woman, behold thy son," He seems to say, "Thou art the New Eve; I am thy first-born son. My mission being accomplished, I return to the Father; but this son of thy faith [St. John] and My love has not yet fulfilled the mission. August Woman, Spouse of thy first-born in the work of regeneration, behold I confide him to you."

We are then, in very truth, the children of Mary. We belong to her as a child belongs to its mother. In her and through her, Jesus Christ, in communicating to us His life, has made us partakers of His nature, so that we are born spiritually of Mary in consequence of her ineffable union with Jesus Christ, the Father of our souls.

When Jesus said to His well-beloved disciple, "Behold thy Mother," Mary was already his Mother; she had already given birth to him. The name of the disciple is not indicated because he represents all men. Therefore the Blessed Virgin is our Mother not only because she has adopted us for children, but she is our Mother according to the full force of the term because she has brought us forth spiritually just as she really gave birth to Jesus Christ.

Jesus Christ in the womb of Mary prepared her by a profusion of grace to be the Mother of His Mystical Body as she was the Mother of His natural body; for He wished that we receive from her the life of the Spirit as He had received from her the life of the body; that we depend upon her for the maintenance and growth of our spiritual life, as He depended upon her for the maintenance and growth of His corporal life.

Mary is really the Mother of Christians, the Mother of the predestined, the Mother of the disciples of Jesus Christ. As Jesus Christ has been conceived in the virginal womb of Mary according to nature by the operation of the Holy Spirit, so also all the elect have been conceived according to the Spirit of Faith and Baptism in the womb of the tender charity of Mary. The Christians are the members of the Mystical Body of Jesus Christ, and they make only one Jesus Christ so that each Christian can say "Born of the Virgin Mary." What a powerful means we have for coming to the resemblance of Jesus Christ to have for Mother the very Mother of Jesus Christ.

V. MARY AT THE CROSS ON CALVARY

Up until the time of Father Chaminade, if spiritual writers attempted to explain the Spiritual Maternity of Mary, they used the third and fourth words of Christ on the cross as their proof. For

Father Chaminade the words of Christ, "Behold thy son" and "Behold thy Mother," took on a new and special meaning. He wanted to emphasize the suffering that Mary also endured in becoming our Mother. Also he drew from this greatest moment the unity of the Mystical Body in as much as St. John represented all of us. Finally, for Father Chaminade, the words of Christ were the last will and testament to a fact already realized, a solemn announcement to emphasize the greatness of the Spiritual Maternity was called for.

The Father associated Mary in the fecundity of His love and the Son associated her in the fecundity of His sufferings. Thus she is our Mother (1) by a maternal love and (2) by her fruitful sufferings which tore her soul on Calvary.

She becomes the Mother of Christians in this sense that she engenders them at the foot of the cross although she was already their Mother by her Divine Maternity. . . . Oh, how fortunate for us was that stroke which pierced her soul with the sword of sorrow; it has given birth to the family of the elect.

If we admire the charity of Mary in the consent, in the Fiat that she gave in the mystery of the Incarnation, let us remember how many times has she given this consent since she had the happiness of becoming our Mother? She renewed it in some way every instant of her life. You see the sorrow of Mary only at the time of the Passion and you overlook the fact that the sacrifice of Calvary is for Mary, as for Jesus Christ, only the consummation of a sacrifice begun at the Incarnation.

*   *   *

Jesus at the time of His death gave His divine Mother to St. John for Mother. It is on Calvary and on the cross that He gives her. It is one of the most important clauses of His testament. . . . Jesus looks upon the gift that He is going to bequeath — it is His own Mother — and the person to whom He is going to make the bequest — it is the disciple — who was standing and whom Jesus loved.

Would we not also be justified in saying that He wished to delay His revelation of the maternity of Mary until the day on which the Virgin at the foot of the cross showed in such an admirable way that she was our Mother by sacrificing her first-born Son and God for our salvation?

He said to His Mother, "Woman, behold your son." Jesus speaks first to His Mother. Mary accepts, Mary conceives us, and Jesus immediately informs the well-beloved disciple that Mary has engendered him, that she is his Mother.

For the children of Mary what a consoling declaration is this which Jesus pronounces on the cross: "Behold thy Mother." It operates exactly what it signifies.

The Blessed Virgin felt the force of the words of her Son; she was the co-operator in the great mystery of the Redemption; and by it she was really engendering us at the foot of the cross. Mary understood then, that she was as the term of this consummation in unity, in order that her Son and all His disciples together with Him should form only one Son, as she, her Son, and all the disciples in perfect unity, make up only one Body of Christ. This is the doctrine of Jesus Christ.

Jesus gives the name of "woman" to His Mother. It was the name which the old prophecy, accomplished by Jesus Christ, gave to her. She was aware of the accomplishment and she had a great part in it, though her association in it was due to grace . . . Mary is witness of how her Son crushed the head of the serpent, while the serpent, deceived by his own artifices, congratulates himself on having crushed the heel, that is, that which is closest to the earth and the weakest in His humanity.

In speaking to His Mother, Christ says, "Woman," and not Mother, in order to derobe Himself, as it were, of His quality of Son. Woman, instead of Mary or another title, to avoid all that would in any way soften the bitterness of her sorrow; Woman par excellence, the true Eve, the only true Mother of the living.

It is, then, at the moment of the most cruel separation that Jesus wished to be replaced by ourselves in the esteem and affection of His Mother, and Mary. Consenting in this substitution which was almost equally generous on the part of the Son, who asked for it, and the part of the Mother who accepted it, Mary adopted us all at once as the children of her immense charity.

Jesus was her Son and her love for such an amiable Son is easily imagined. On Calvary Jesus seems to order her to transfer all the affection that she had for Him to His disciple, for He wishes that she regard him as her Son. "Behold your son." Mary loved St. John out of love for Jesus Christ in the same way that she loves Jesus Christ Himself.

St. John is the only one of whom our Lord spoke, in order to mark the unity of the elect. St. John represents all of them in his person. All the elect are to form one with Christ. With Christ, one Christ. Jesus Christ is the Head of this Mystical Body.

St. John had already been instructed concerning the profound mystery of the union and of the consummation in unity; but until the descent of the Holy Ghost, he may have understood only the happiness of possessing the Blessed Virgin, to whom he was so strongly and piously devoted, and it is for this reason no doubt, that he only adds, "And from that hour, he accepted her as his own."

It is most worthy of belief that St. John, the beloved disciple, realized the inestimable value of the treasure which had been confided to him in the person of Mary. Beside himself with joy and gratitude, he names himself and explains to us the vision under whose form he had conceived the grandeur of Mary in her Immaculate Conception (cf. Apoc. 12:1–18).

Who would not truly say that St. John was more favored in these circumstances than the other disciples even though they were all represented? How can we think that Mary would not always have a special predilection for St. John, and, it can be said, a love for him greater than the others?

St. John was the disciple of Jesus Christ, but he was also a priest and bishop. It is thus that St. John represented the entire Church, the faithful and their pastors. Thus Mary is the Mother of the Church. . . . It is only as a disciple of Jesus Christ that St. John becomes the son of the most pure Mary. But St. John represents all the faithful. . . . St. John is attached to Christ in a general sense according to his position as a disciple, but he is attached to Him in a more special sense according to his position as a priest.

Now what is it that procured this favor for St. John? It is his fidelity in following Jesus Christ humiliated. It is due to the fact that he was the well-beloved disciple of Jesus. Our love for Jesus Christ and our constancy in following Him in poverty and self-renunciation are then the assurance of a special protection on the part of Mary.

But observe that if St. John here represents all Christians, it can only be faithful Christians. Jesus spoke to the disciple whom He loved. Now, how can sinners who do not wish to love God and who do nothing in order to be loved by Him, how, I say, can they consider those words as addressed to themselves?

St. John understood what this favor was, receiving Mary as Mother; God had given him the understanding of it. St. John, who specially loved chastity, had been enlightened in a special way. We do not see any saint or any prophet who penetrated so profoundly the depths of the mysteries of the designs of God as St. John.

* * *

Just as the life of the Redeemer is one of suffering, consummated by the offering of His very life on Calvary, so too the life of Mary is a faithful copy of her Son's in her humility as well as in her sufferings. She no sooner pronounced these words, "Behold the handmaid of the Lord, be it done unto me according to thy word," than her days started to become days of pain, of sorrows, and of bitterness.

The entire Passion was impressed upon this incomparable Mother. She experienced all the interior and corporal sufferings of her Son in her soul as well as in her body in order that she might be as conformed with Him as possible.

The Blessed Virgin has so great a resemblance with her divine Son, both in His virtues and in His Passion, because Jesus Christ gave her a new being of grace for the humanity He received from her. As Mother of God she is above all other creatures, not only by the eminence of this august calling, but also by this new being of grace which allowed her to penetrate the interior operations of her Son, to imitate them, and to experience in them all that Jesus Christ experienced in Himself and so by them to become the faithful copy of Him. Thus it is that she is associated in all

His mysteries. Thus it is that she comes to Calvary to suffer as Coredemptrix and to bear in sorrow the children of the new Church.

It was willed that she should join herself to the Eternal Father and that, for the salvation of sinners, they should by a mutual agreement deliver their common Son to the torture. . . . It is also at this time that she receives her fecundity. Woman, behold thy Son. She is the Eve of the New Alliance . . . what a sacrifice she has made! What love! Would she give up her divine Son for us if she did not love us as her children?

In the presence of the holy women at the foot of the cross, there is nothing which is not according to the law of grace, and even of nature. But that Mary, the Mother of Jesus, should be present — here we see the Strong Woman, the Mother of Sorrows, who receives in her heart all the blows which pierced the heart of her Son; here we see a mystery of incomprehensible love. Mary is at the foot of the cross as advocate of the human race and Mother of the elect.

She had felt in herself all the pain of the nails, and the terrible sufferings that her Son had experienced on the cross; and now she only had to receive the deadly transfixion which was to take away the life of the very author of life, in order to suffer all the horrors of death. She received this transfixion by the hands of the executioners, who pierced at one and the same time the heart of Jesus and the heart of His Mother.

It is at the foot of the cross that this divine Mother gave birth to us at the moment that her divine Son was going to expire. At that moment her soul suffered the same suffering as her divine Son. Then was accomplished the first prophecy that God had made when He said to the woman, "You shall give birth in sorrow." And then He cursed the serpent. He told him that there would be between him and the children of the Woman an irreconcilable hatred.

O how painful this mortal transfixion must have been for Mary! St. Bernard says that it was more painful for the Mother than for the Son, since the Son received what He desired — death; and the Mother was unable to obtain what she wished, to die out of love for her Son. Where can we find a person who has suffered so much as Mary?

She knows, by the Son whom she is immolating and by the very fact of her immolation, as by the sacrifice of the Incarnation, that she is the Mother of the human race, whose salvation is in the death of Jesus. She wishes, then, the death of Jesus, because she wills the life of the human race.

* * *

Is it not beyond all doubt that at the moment that the Blessed Virgin saw the executioners preparing to crucify her adorable Son, that she offered Him to God, as being not only the Son of God, but also her own Son and because by her title of Mother, she had rights and authorities over Him?

This prayer then Mary addressed to the Eternal Father on Calvary in which she offered to Him for the redemption of the world her Son as her own belonging by the maternal right that she possessed. "My Lord and my God. You are the Father of Your only Son, who by the eternal generation is born true God of true God. . . . And by the temporal generation in which He suffers. I nourished Him with my own milk. As a mother I love Him as the best Son who has ever been born of a creature, and in this quality of mother, I have a natural right to His most holy humanity in the Personality that He has, and Your Divine Providence never refuses any right, which belongs to anyone.

"Therefore I offer up to You this right of my maternity and I place Him once more in Your hands so that Your Son and mine may be sacrificed for the redemption of the human race. O Lord, accept this offering, since I could not offer You as much if I myself were crucified, not only because my Son is really God, and of the same substance as You, but also because of my sorrow, for if I died and our destinies were changed, so that His holy life would be preserved, that would not be a great consolation for me nor the accomplishment of my desires."

This thought of Mary's giving birth to us in her sorrow is a consoling one for the faithful disciple. What is there that he has to be afraid of? Mary would remind Jesus Christ that this is a son whom He has given her; she would show Him the suffering which His spiritual birth has caused her. Throwing herself at the feet of the cross of her Son, she would beseech Him not to pierce her heart with a new sword of sorrow in depriving her forever of the son whom He has given her.

Therefore, to be the Mother of God is to be the Coredemptrix of men; it is to be a cause of the salvation of the universe; it is to furnish the blood which has been poured out for us on the cross; it is to form the adorable Body which has served for the ransom of the human race; it is to produce from the best of oneself the victim which is to appease an irate God.

At three o'clock in the afternoon all shall transport themselves in spirit to Mount Calvary in order there to contemplate the Heart of Mary, their tender Mother, pierced by a sword of sorrow, and to recall the happy moment in which they have been born anew. Mary conceived us at Nazareth, but it was on Calvary, at the foot of the cross of Jesus dying, that she gave us birth. This is the motive that ought to enlist all the children of the divine Mother for this reunion of heart and spirit on Calvary at three o'clock. At this hour all shall suspend or interrupt their occupation of the moment, if they can do so without inconvenience; those who are alone shall kneel down.

The following prayer Father Chaminade composed for his spiritual children to be said at three o'clock each afternoon.

O divine Jesus, we transport ourselves in spirit to Mount Calvary, to ask pardon for our sins, which are the cause of Thy death. We thank Thee for having thought of us in that solemn moment, and for having made us children of Thy own Mother. Holy Virgin, show thyself our Mother by taking us under thy special protection. St. John, be our patron and model, and obtain for us the grace of imitating thy filial devotion to Mary, our Mother. Amen.

May the Father, Son, and Holy Spirit be glorified in all places through the Immaculate Virgin Mary. Amen.

VI. MARY, OUR QUEEN AND MEDIATRIX

For Father Chaminade, Mary's prerogative of mediation between Christ and mankind was a most logical conclusion after proclaiming

Mary our Mother from the cross. Mary does more than approve
the graces of the Redemption as applied to souls, as the less bold
theologians spoke, but as the most recent popes have taught, Mary
has a real part in the distribution of Christ's merits. Father Chaminade taught as the popes that Mary is truly our Mother who ob-
tains whatever is necessary for our salvation. Only the delinquent
children refuse what their beloved mother knows they need. If we
need it, Mary has it to give us. Christ has given Mary that prerogative in the economy of our salvation.

As Christ is Mediator between God and us, so it is a part of
the divine plan that Mary be the mediator between Christ and us.

Since the new alliance concluded between heaven and sealed with
the blood of Jesus Christ, God the Father recognizes only His Son,
loves only His Son, and adopts us only in His Son, who is our
elder Brother. All that we offer Him by other hands than those
of His Son will not be agreeable to Him, for it is His Son alone
that He has established as our pontiff and mediator. We must,
then, be united to Christ to go to God. But how are we to unite
ourselves to the Son if not by the mediation of His Mother, deposi-
tary of His vestments, that is, of the merits of her First-Born.

Mary has been constituted by her own Son from the height of
the cross our Mother and Protector. It is in her hands that He has
deposited the treasures of His grace, so that we believe her to be
the natural and constituted Mediatrix between her Son and men,
as the Son is the necessary Mediator between God and men. No
one can go to the Son but by Mary as no one can go to the Father
but by the Son.

How is it possible to find Jesus without Mary since Jesus Himself did not come to us except with the consent of Mary! We reach
Jesus but through Mary, as Jesus came to us but through Mary
and because of this great truth we should desire naught but to
make known to all nations this path, so sure, to reach heaven.

The eternal decree of the wisdom of God concerning Mary He
will never revoke. The gifts of God and His vocation are without
repentance. Here is our process of reasoning: God from all eternity
in the counsels of His wisdom predestined Mary to be the Mother

of the Savior of the world, or to be the organ of the Incarnation, the universal principle of grace. This choice is a gift of God, infinitely glorious for Mary. But the gifts of God are without repentance. Therefore, this choice will rest forever. All the graces that men receive are only the applications of the operations of the grace of the Incarnation.

For a Mediatrix two qualities are necessary to establish this title. A sovereign power over the person who is to be influenced, is necessary, and an extreme goodness toward men, in order to employ this goodness in their favor. Now the quality of Mother of God necessarily includes these two characteristics as two inseparable properties.

No one can go to the Son except by Mary as no one can go to the Father except by the Son. The mediation of Jesus Christ is of faith. If that of Mary is not defined by the Church, it is taught by the generality of the doctors so that it approaches closely to faith and he would be temerarious who would dare to deny it.

We can have life only by Jesus Christ and in Jesus Christ. Now it is by Mary that this life is communicated to us. Thus St. Bernard tells us formally that God does not wish that we should receive any grace that has not passed by the hands of Mary. The doctrine of Suarez, who carefully examined the spirit of the Church in regard to the devotion toward the Blessed Virgin, goes so far as to conclude that the Church believes that the intercession of the Most Blessed Virgin is useful and necessary.

It is and will always be true that, having once received by Mary the universal principle of grace, we will receive by her intercession the diverse applications of that grace in all the states of the Christian life. Her charity, having contributed so much to our salvation in the mystery of the Incarnation, which is the universal principle of grace, she will contribute eternally in all the other operations of grace which are only consequences of it.

The sublime words of the holy Doctor, St. Bernard, do not appear adequate to us in order to give a complete idea of the maternal tenderness of Mary. It seems to us that we must add that she has not given us her Son conditionally, but absolutely; not for a time, but forever. She was not content to give us her Son

once, but she gives Him to us whenever we ask her for Him. . . .
We must say that if we are willing, Mary continually engenders
her Son in us. She gives Him to us at every moment by communicating to us the graces which He has merited by His death.

What confidence we should have in Mary because she is all-
powerful! Not that she can do everything herself, but because she
is able to obtain everything from her Son.

We do not pretend that much is to be expected of men; on
the contrary, we acknowledge that all our help is in the name of
the Lord, with whom the Blessed Virgin Mary, His divine Mother,
is our great intermediary; we look upon men merely as the objects
upon whom we can fully exercise our charity.

Praying in union with Jesus Christ is a condition without which
we can obtain nothing. What do we mean by saying in union
with Jesus Christ? It is to pray in Him, with Him, and by Him.
Second, we must do so (so that we may be able to unite ourselves
with Jesus Christ) in union with the Blessed Virgin. . . . Jesus
Christ, the Author of all grace, is in the Blessed Virgin; you unite
yourselves to Him in the Blessed Virgin. Jesus Christ presents
our prayers to God, but not immediately as we pronounce them.
They pass by the hands of the Blessed Virgin, who asks for us.
The greater our faith, the more quickly does our prayer arrive.

The Gospel teaches us that the three kinds of grace which God
gives to men have been accorded at the request of Mary. The
grace of a vocation at the wedding feast of Cana, the grace of
justification at the sanctification of St. John, perseverance in grace
by the legacy of Jesus Christ on the cross that gave the beloved
disciple to Mary as son.

Christ's greatest operations in the working out of His plan took
place only by the mediation of Mary, operations such as the sanctification of the holy precursor, St. John the Baptist, and the miracle
of the wedding feast of Cana which revealed Him to His disciples
as Son of God.

Jesus Christ wished that the Blessed Virgin after her death should
be the governess of His Mystical Body, of His Church, of His
members, of all the faithful, and the guardian of all His treasures
of graces.

Today Mary exercises in heaven those powers which she did not wish to use on earth. She enters into all her rights. She is established under Christ as Mediator of the faithful, the Channel of grace, the Hope and Mainstay of the Church, the Refuge of sinners, the Protectress of the just, the Resource of nations and empires, the Queen of heaven and earth.

CHAPTER TWO

Consecration to Mary

I. IN WHAT IT CONSISTS

From his thorough study of the Spiritual Maternity of Mary, Father Chaminade developed his devotion to Mary. Devotion to Mary was more than pious prayers and wearing of scapulars; it was a dedication of a whole life in thought, word, and deed. In short, devotion to Mary was a cult, that is, a cult or culture which was the way one set his whole life to revolve about Mary for Mary, and by Mary, always remembering that he is a son of Mary. All his thoughts, actions, and words were those of a son of Mary and always a son of Mary. Father Chaminade called this guiding principle that determined the devotion to Mary filial piety or filial devotion. It is the love and devotion that a son or daughter demonstrates for his or her mother and father. Father Chaminade asked his disciples to look at Mary's love toward God the Father. This he pointed out was filial devotion. In our love for God we have none better than Mary to imitate. He then asked them to look at Christ's love for Mary, because Mary was His Mother. Christ set the example of our love and veneration of Mary. There is no better example to imitate, and this is filial devotion to Mary. Herein lies the teaching of Father Chaminade. His whole spirituality that he offers his spiritual sons and daughters revolves about this momentous principle of filial devotion.

Not to recognize Mary in the mysteries of Jesus Christ is to betray our ignorance of the whole economy of religion. Christ has so ordained all concerns of religion so that Mary participated and co-operated in all of them. If any proof were wanted, we need only to mention that Mary is the Mother of Jesus and of all those that are born of Jesus. All the graces we receive from Jesus pass through the hands of Mary and are at her disposal. Does not Jesus, by this very fact, furnish us an additional proof of His incomparable love for mankind? The best and richest of fathers thus prepares the means of our salvation. Through the hands of the most tender Mother He applies these means to us. Having thus placed all the treasures of His grace in the hands of Mary, He shows His intention of having us always apply for them to her. Our confidence in her reverts to His honor and glory. We should therefore find no difficulty in replying to the question: What is the extent of the veneration due to Mary?

Devotion to the Blessed Virgin is, therefore, that love which leads us with promptitude, diligence, and eagerness to imitate the Blessed Virgin, to wait upon her every desire, to practice and spread the veneration due to her. A genuine and sound devotion to the Blessed Virgin implies the imitation of her virtues. "Now therefore, my children, hear me: blessed are they that keep my ways" (Prov. 8:32).

Keeping all things in proportion to serve God as did Mary is in equivalent terms to serve Him as did Jesus Christ. Grace in forming Mary has taken as model Jesus Christ and the august Virgin is perfect and agreeable to the eyes of God only because of this resemblance. She is as an exact imitation as it was possible to be with Him who is eternally the object of the pleasure of the Most High. To imitate Mary is the surest, promptest, and easiest way toward imitating Jesus Christ.

Our devotion to the august Mother should comprise a high and loving esteem of her perfection, a full and unlimited confidence based upon her powerful influence with God and her tender interest in our welfare, an ardent zeal to advance her honor, to spread her worship and to exalt her prerogatives. If to these sentiments we join the practice of her virtues, we shall truly merit the title of "Child of Mary," as well as all the beneficences of her power.

Those who have no devotion to Mary nor love her may well fear lest the faith in them is dead. For how can we not love what, after God, is the most amiable being in existence?

We have all been conceived in Mary; we must also be born of her and formed by her to the likeness of Jesus Christ. In view of this principle, what confidence ought we not to have in Mary for the acquisition, little by little, from her and through her, of the traits of conformity with Jesus Christ effected by the Spirit of Jesus Christ.

In whatever time and in whatever epoch of life we may enter into the heart of this good Mother, we never find other interests save those of the Sacred Heart of Jesus Christ, her First Born and our elder Brother. The love of Mary for us is so ardent, it is furthermore so related to our conformity with her divine Son, that all her ambition, if we can use this term for the most saintly of creatures, is that the children conceived by her charity, after this adorable Savior, make with Him but one and the same son.

It is of Mary that Jesus is born. He was nourished and reared by her; He never separated Himself from her during the entire course of His temporal life; He was subject to her; He has associated her in all His labors, in all His sorrows, in all His mysteries. Devotion to Mary, therefore, is then one of the most outstanding points in the imitation of Jesus Christ.

Mary does not limit her maternal care to the preservation and maintenance of the life of grace within us, which we have received from Jesus Christ through her. But she also at the same time is constantly striving to make us more and more conformable to Jesus, our divine Model. Even though we are called to the glory of resembling the Divinity by the privilege of our regeneration in Baptism, we shall not be saved as St. Paul says, except insofar as the Father finds us conformable to the image of Jesus Christ.

To tend incessantly to one's proper sanctification is the first object comprised in the design to resemble Mary and imitate Jesus Christ. Here is the place where one works at becoming a saint. For is there a virtue, a degree of perfection which is not dear to Mary and which she did not attain in order to conform herself to her divine Son? Who has accomplished better the precept: "Be perfect as your heavenly Father is perfect"?

All those who would live a real and active life as a child of Mary must model themselves according to Jesus Christ in the maternal womb of Mary's goodness as Jesus was there formed according to our nature. In other words, to strive for the most sublime perfection, that is, to live the life of Jesus Christ under the auspices of Mary.

*   *   *

If the devotion to Mary is genuine, it will lead to a consecration to Mary, no doubt a public consecration. When Father Chaminade spoke of consecration, he visualized as many degrees of it as there are different states of life. Thus he spoke of consecration to Mary for first communicants, for school children in sodalities, for lay groups and the highest form of consecration — that of professing vows in religious life for the glory of God and for the honor of Mary.

What is the meaning of consecrating oneself to Mary? It is to believe and to confess the eminent prerogatives which flow from the supreme dignity of Mother of God. It is to attach, to dedicate, to devote oneself without any reserve to the unique worship which is her due.

We consecrate ourselves because we are convinced that we shall not bring men back to Jesus except it be through His most holy Mother, whom the Doctors of the Church acclaim as being our only Hope, our Mother, our Refuge, our Help, our Strength, and our Life.

A sincere consecration to the most pure Mary forms a true alliance between the person consecrating himself and the Blessed Mother. On the one hand, the august Mary takes under her most powerful protection the soul who casts himself into the hands of her maternal tenderness. On the other hand, the child of Mary contracts with Mary the most sweet and loving obligations.

Let everyone always remember what we professed by this act of consecration. We promised that Mary deserves a special veneration which is due to none but her; that she is the Queen of the world, the Queen of men and angels, the Channel of all graces; that, in contracting with Mary an alliance which is as intimate as that between mother and child, they have also bound themselves to certain duties.

We have bound ourselves to Mary. For what purpose? To act as a child would toward a loving mother; to love her, to honor, to obey her, to assist her. Oh, yes, especially to this last effect of filial love — assistance, active benevolence. We undertake to proclaim her glory everywhere.

In his individual life, this consecration must extend its influence even to the very motives and intentions which direct his actions. He will apply himself unceasingly to purify them. He will begin and end all his work with a prayer. He will give his work vitality and carry it on by placing himself often under the eyes of his august Protector, by pronouncing the sweet and tender name of Mary, or by singing her praises.

Fortunate indeed, a thousand times fortunate are those who, not content with belonging to Mary as other men, have consecrated themselves to her, body and soul, and have made themselves in a particular way her sons and daughters. Her heart throbs with joy and love when she beholds them enrolling under her standard. She manifests for them a tenderness of preference and predilection. She lavishes upon them profusely the treasures of grace and of faith. She invites them more frequently to the sacred banquet of the Lamb. She inspires the Church to open for them the precious storehouse of the indulgences for their least acts of piety. She watches over them with every particular care and she obeys their wishes somewhat as God yields to the voice of the just. She accords everything to them, whatever they petition for themselves and for others — even miracles.

In a manual that Father Chaminade drew up for those who have consecrated themselves in a special way, he listed seven so-termed rules. These rules were kept in general terms so that they could be applicable to everyone, depending on his vocation in life.

First obligation. A child of Mary invokes the assistance of his kind and powerful Mother in all spiritual and temporal needs, in all dangers of soul and body, and especially when he comes to the moment of choosing his state of life.

Second obligation. He performs, with the respect and veneration demanded by her sublime dignity, all the duties relating to her worship. This respect and veneration is demanded in return for the protection which Mary continuously lavishes upon her children of predilection.

Third obligation. The adopted child of this divine Mother will be careful not to engage in anything which might harm her interests. What a strange contradiction there would be between a real consecration to Mary and a line of conduct opposed to the interests of her glory.

Fourth obligation. The strongest obligation contracted by this filial devotion is imitation of the virtues of which Mary has given the example to the world. To be under the patronage of the holiest of virgins is equivalent to making a public profession of combating all bad habits. To act differently would be to profane the holy name of Mary and to render oneself unworthy of her favors.

Fifth obligation. The child of Mary will never go to sleep in the state of mortal sin. He will take immediate steps to withdraw from this state, if he should have had the misfortune to fall into it.

Sixth obligation. A sixth effect imposed by this sacred alliance will prompt the child of the august Mother to favor everything that might contribute to her honor — such as prayers, public and private devotions, erections of shrines, celebration of her feasts in her honor, etc.

Seventh obligation. St. Joseph, the spouse of Mary most pure, will always hold a prominent place in their hearts. Since in a way they belong to his holy and amiable family, they will pay him a particular homage of respect and confidence.

I am astonished at the graces and blessings received by those who sincerely make the *Act of Consecration* to Mary and who persevere in the disposition which have inspired them to take such a step. Oh, how happy are the true children of Mary! The Mother of Jesus truly becomes their Mother in the fullest meaning of the word.

The following prayer is the act of consecration Father Chaminade gave to all those who consecrated themselves to Mary. He asked that they recite it attentively each morning and evening and to meditate upon it from time to time.

Glorious Queen of heaven and earth, at the foot of thy throne where respect and love have enchained our hearts, we offer thee our homage of service and praise, we consecrate ourselves to thy worship, and with joy embrace a state of life where everything is done under thy protection, and everyone pledges himself to praise thee, to serve thee, to proclaim thy greatness, and to defend thy Immaculate Conception. Would that, by our zeal for the honor of thy veneration and the interests of thy glory, we were able to make amends to thee for all the assaults of heresy, the outrages of unbelief, and the indifferences and neglect of the greater part of mankind.

O Mother of our Redeemer, Dispenser of all graces, extend the empire of religion in the souls of men, banish error, preserve and increase the faith in this country, protect innocence, preserve it from the dangers of this world and from the allurements of sin. Mindful of our necessities and favorable to our desires, obtain for us the charity which animates the just, the virtues which sanctify, and the glory which crowns them. Amen.

II. LOVE OF MARY OUR MOTHER

God having called her to this glorious ministry does not wish that she should be a mere channel for such a grace, but on the contrary, a voluntary instrument contributing to this great work not only by her excellent dispositions, but also, and especially by a movement of her will. It is her charity.

The charity of Mary was in some way the fruitful source from which grace started its flow and spread abundantly over all of human nature.

But who can understand the height, the width, the depth of this ocean of charity? Who would be able to understand how much she wishes to enrich us with spiritual goods? Who would be able to understand the evils that she wishes to deliver us from? Under every aspect she shares in the dispositions and sentiments of the adorable heart of her divine Son who is Himself the God of love.

Since Satan unceasingly persecutes the Church of Jesus Christ, how can those whose main purpose in life is to uphold it expect to be free from his assaults? Most of all this does apply to the avowed children of Mary who are expressly bound in coalition against the empire of Satan. Are we not fully panoplied in the might of the prime prophecy uttered against the serpent: "I will put enmities between thee and the woman, between thy seed and her seed; she shall crush thy head" (Gen. 3:15).

In our own day the great prevailing heresy is religious indifference which blunts the souls of men, and reduces them to a state of torpid egoism and of moral degeneration. The depths of the infernal abyss are ejecting dense clouds of black and pestilential smoke which threaten to envelop the whole world in a dark night, devoid of good and full of evil, a darkness that is impervious, as it were, to the life-giving rays of the Sun of Justice. The divine torch of faith is burning low and dying in the heart of Christianity; virtue is becoming more and more rare and is disappearing, while vice is rampant and spreading with terrifying fury. It seems that the time is near when we are to witness what has been foretold, a general defection and an all but universal apostasy.

And yet, this sad but true picture of our times does not by any means discourage us. Mary's power has not been diminished. It is our firm belief that she will subdue this heresy like all the rest, for she is today as she ever was, the incomparable woman, the woman of promise who is to crush the head of the infernal serpent. Jesus Himself, who in His public utterances always addressed her by this great name, would thereby teach us that she is the hope, the joy, and the life of the Church and the terror of hell. To her, therefore, is reserved a great victory in our day, for to her belongs the glory of saving the faith from the destruction with which it is being threatened.

Every period in the history of the Church has its record of the combats and the glorious victories of the august Mother of God. Ever since the Lord has sown dissension between her and the serpent, she has constantly vanquished the world and the powers of hell. All the heresies, the Church tells us, have been subdued by the Blessed Virgin Mary, and little by little she has reduced them to the silence of oblivion.

Discover that Mary is to be glorified from one century to another, but more especially in these latter days, by the visible and almost tangible protection which she extends over Holy Church which always demonstrates her greatness and the power of her protection.

Let us entrust all to the protection of Mary to whom her divine Son has reserved the last victories over hell. Let us be, in all humility, my dear children, the heel of the Woman.

Our dependence upon the august Mary is universal. If we could be independent of her in any matter, the solicitude which her maternal love gives for us would be contradicted on this point and this would be repugnant to the idea that we have of the works of love, of gratitude, and of obedience which her divine Son has operated in her.

It is incontestable that, among all the elect, Mary enjoys preeminence in the power of her intercession for us. Can it be that she no longer takes interest in us? "The greater the assurance of the saints of their own happiness, the greater is their concern about our salvation" (St. Cyprian). Is she not endowed with the power? She was so endowed upon earth. Can it be that she knows not our needs? The angels know them. Would invoking her seem disparaging to a higher worship? We do not go to Mary as our God, but we go to God through Mary, as faith tells us that He came to us through her.

What crushes our hope? Fear of the judgments of God and the sight of our sins. But, in the first place, Mary is an all-powerful advocate with our Judge. She is our advocate with her Son, as St. Bernard says, as Jesus is our advocate with His Heavenly Father; and, second, according to the same saint, a characteristic of Mary is to be singularly the Mother of sinners. Is it not to sinners that she owes her crowning glory, since in the case that there were no sinners she would never have been Mother of God?

The great means of success is to empty yourself of self-seeking and to abandon yourself unreservedly into the hands of God. From this double point of view the protection of Mary will prove most useful to you. The Blessed Virgin and our Savior, with whom we must ever remain united, will supply for your weakness and for the lack of stability in your mind. Turn to Mary and beseech her to show herself your Mother by showing you her Son. Proceed, my dear Son, with never failing courage and great confidence in the Most Blessed Virgin. She is really your good Mother; prove yourself really her son, in mind and heart.

III. UNION OF JESUS AND MARY

"One has only to recall all the mysteries of Jesus Christ and one finds Mary associated with them. Mary has a part in all the joyous, sorrowful, and glorious mysteries of Christ." In these words, Father Chaminade succinctly summarizes his whole thought on the most perfect union of two souls on this earth and in heaven. We speak of a mystical soul's union with Christ, but the union of Mary was far beyond that. Christ chose Mary to be so united with Him that all his actions for our redemption were the result of intimate collaboration. By this union Mary became our Coredemptrix, our Mediatrix, and our Queen.

Father Chaminade speaks of the mysteries of Christ and of Mary. Ordinarily we think of the word "mystery" as a truth of our faith. By the mysteries of Christ, Father Chaminade meant the actions of Christ intended for our salvation, and the graces that are connected with and merited by these actions, which are thereby spiritual or mysterious. These graces we receive whenever in union with Christ we perform a deed similar to a deed performed by Christ while on earth. There is a grace for every state of life, for every action in life, for every contingency in life, for every difficult moment in life.

But the mystery of Mary is inseparably bound up with the mystery of Christ. Hence, whatever we do because of Christ, we do for Mary also, because Christ has united Mary in all His mysteries.

Thus the union of Jesus and Mary, for Father Chaminade meant more than a virtue to be admired and imitated. It was for him the means of reaching a full maturity in spiritual growth. Because of the union of Jesus and Mary we have our salvation and the means to make ourselves worthy of that redemption.

Jesus Christ associates His Mother most intimately with Himself in the great work of the regeneration of the human race. In following the story of the Redemption as told in Sacred Scripture, we find the Son "with Mary, his Mother." After the sin in the Garden of Eden the Woman who will crush the head of the

serpent is promised at the same time as the Redeemer. The prophets
of old, when speaking of the Savior, do not fail to make mention
of His Mother. . . .

When the time had come for the realization of the mysteries
foretold by the prophets, the co-operation of Mary and her association with her divine Son in the role of the New Eve is evident
beyond all doubt. Without mentioning the Incarnation and the
birth of the Savior, because the active co-operation of Mary in those
mysteries is too evident, let us take a rapid glance at the various
instances connected with the life and death of our Savior. When
the Magi come to adore Him, they find Him on His Mother's
knees. We see Him in the arms of Mary when fleeing into Egypt
to escape the jealous fury of a cruel king. At the painful ceremony
of the circumcision, Mary is there, accepting with loving resignation, for the salvation of mankind, the sword of sorrow that is to
pierce her heart. Mary carries Him to the temple, presents Him
to the high priest, and offers herself with Him to the heavenly
Father.

Then follow thirty years of most intimate and loving family
life, spent in the sweetest converse of Mother and Son, both doing
the will of the Father in silent recollection and obscure labor,
sharing their joys, their fatigues, their watchings, and their prayers.
Next come the three short years of the Savior's public life, beginning with His first miracle at the marriage of Cana, at the request
of His Mother. She, too, shares with Him the trying days of His
apostolic career. Everywhere Mary is with Jesus, associated with
Him in His labors and privations, her Mother's heart bleeding at
the ill treatment He received from His own ungrateful people.

It is especially in connection with the Passion of our Lord
that the sacred writers are careful to note Mary's participation in
all the mysteries of the sufferings and death of Jesus, her Son.

As it was necessary "that Christ should suffer and thus enter
into His glory," so also was it necessary that Mary, His august
Mother, should suffer with Him in order to effect, conjointly with
Him, our regeneration to the life of grace. Thus we see Mary in
spirit in the praetorium at the time of Christ's trial before Pilate,
at the court of the high priest, and on the bloodstained road to

Calvary. Again we find Mary standing at the foot of the cross, sharing every pang of anguish and of mortal pain with Jesus, her dying Son.

Let us not imagine for a single moment, that when her heart was crushed with unutterable sorrow, that most tender of mothers should so far forget her sublime mission as to endeavor to save her divine Son from the horrors of a most painful and infamous death. No, indeed, for she, too, accepts the cross, she wishes it for Jesus, she desires it for herself. "More submissive even than Abraham," says St. Antoninus, "she would, were it necessary, with her own hands have plunged the deicide steel into the bosom of her beloved Isaac, because she so perfectly desired the accomplishment of the divine will." In truth, Mary knew full well that by the Son whom she immolated, and by the fact of the Sacrifice itself, and likewise by that of the Incarnation, she had become the Mother of mankind, whose salvation was to be accomplished by the death of Jesus, her Son. Therefore she desired His death, because she desired the life of the human race.

But Mary's exalted mission does not end on Calvary. Her charity, stronger than sorrow and death, enables her to survive an ordeal that would have crushed a thousand lives less fragile than her own. For is she not the New Eve and, as such, necessary to her children? Yes, she must still take part in the glorious mystery of the Resurrection of her first-born Son, and be present, too, at His triumphant Ascension into glory. Then, her presence is required in the midst of the Apostles gathered about her in the Cenacle, while her maternal solicitude must extend over the infant Church, to edify and to instruct the faithful, and to guide them aright along the rugged roads of a pagan world until the day when this earth shall behold her borne by the hands of angels to the highest heavens, next to the eternal throne of her divine Son, Jesus Christ.

Still the sublime Mission of Mary does not end with her entrance into glory. Even in heaven she continues to co-operate in the work of the regeneration, for all things are done through Mary, and every good gift comes to us through her.

Thus we are led to ask: How can we find Jesus without Mary, since Jesus did not wish to come to us without the consent of Mary?

We go to Jesus only by Mary just as Jesus came to us only by her.

Mary's role in the generation of the Mystical Body was of the utmost importance. No one can know the mystery of Jesus Christ who does not see the most pure Mary in the whole economy of religion. Jesus Christ has disposed everything in religion in such a way that the Blessed Virgin has participated and co-operated in it all.

One can say that the entire Mystical Body of Christ was conceived first in Jesus Christ and then in Mary, because Jesus wished that all that happened in Him should happen in His divine Mother so that she should participate in all His mysteries.

For the human body He received from her, Jesus Christ gave her a new being of grace, which allowed her to penetrate the interior operations of her Son, to imitate them, and to experience in them all that Jesus Christ experienced in Himself and so by them she is associated with Him in all His mysteries.

Since perfection consists in conformity with Jesus Christ under the protection and the maternal solicitude of Mary, we must make known more and more the reason why Jesus Christ came into this world; how He is the way, the truth, and the life; how He communicates His Spirit to us; how the Spirit of Jesus Christ makes us live the life of Jesus Christ and leads us to an entire conformity with Jesus Christ.

Jesus Christ practiced all the virtues with the most sublime perfection, but in the accomplishment of His adorable mysteries, the practice of some virtues especially entered, virtues such as His love for the Blessed Virgin, in whose womb He was conceived and dwelt for nine months and of whom He was born, whom He has associated in all His mysteries, whom He made Mother of all those who would be regenerated in Him.

To Mary was confided the care of the Child Jesus and she was also associated in all the states of the life and death, and resurrection of Jesus Christ. The elect, therefore, will arrive at "perfect manhood, the full maturity of Christ," as St. Paul calls it (Eph. 4:13) only insofar as Mary will be in their regard all that she was to Jesus Christ.

Unite yourself, then, more and more to our Lord and to the

Blessed Virgin; always be in union with the Blessed Virgin, especially in your prayers. But this union, be it with our Lord or the Blessed Virgin, should come more from the heart than from the mind. This is that union in which you must put all your confidence against our corrupt nature and against the temptations of the devil.

They will often raise their heart and mind to her and through her to Jesus Christ, her adorable Son and our Master. They will accustom themselves, at the renewal of their actions and throughout them, if they be lengthy, to offer themselves to the glory of Jesus Christ through the hands of Mary, their divine Mother. To be sure, the Blessed Virgin is not in our midst as our Lord is, but she beholds us from her throne in heaven where she holds sway and from there we may well keep united to her.

Although the following words were written to the religious of the Society of Mary which Father Chaminade founded, yet the message is applicable to all, whether religious or lay people.

The interior spirit consists in living in a constant and perfect union with God, by a faithful correspondence with the graces which he daily receives. The heart of a religious must be his oratory, the place of his retreat, his house of prayer. It must be a temple to which he betakes himself frequently in order to offer his humble thanksgiving to God, and to expose to God his own needs and those of our Holy Mother the Church. But the religious of Mary must, in all these exercises, be united with Mary his Mother at all times and everywhere. It is through Mary, with her, and like her that he constantly strives to acquire that state of perfection to which he feels himself called. He entertains the sweet and consoling confidence that he will surely succeed under the protection of his Mother, in choosing her as his patron and model; for he firmly believes that to imitate Mary is to imitate her adorable Son, which is the principal purpose and final end of our glorious vocation.

IV. MISSIONARIES OF MARY

We are our brother's keeper and the divine decree has willed that every man must aid his neighbor in saving his soul. For

Father Chaminade, anyone who truly loved the Blessed Virgin Mary, automatically would become a zealous child of Mary in promoting devotion to Mary and worship of God. All children of Mary are missionaries not that they go to foreign countries, but that they are sent among their neighbors to aid in the salvation of the world.

We are in a particular manner the auxiliaries and the missionaries of the Blessed Virgin in the great work of the reform of morals, and in the preservation and propagation of the Faith; that is to say, in the sanctification of our neighbor. The Blessed Virgin makes us the depositaries of her ingenuity in working out the designs of her almost infinite charity, and we profess to serve her faithfully to the end of our life, and to carry out punctually all that she asks of us. We are happy thus to be able to spend our life and our strength in the service that is due to her.

We are convinced that our particular mission, despite our weakness, is to perform for the welfare of our neighbor all the works of zeal and mercy. To this end we have taken for our motto these words of the Blessed Virgin to the attendants at Cana: "Do whatever he tells you."

Jesus Christ gives you over to Mary to be her faithful minister and her valiant soldier. The King of heaven enrolls you forever in the bodyguard of the Queen. Henceforth you will serve Him by serving her whom He associated in His crown and in His glory, and you shall be in a special manner a soldier and missionary of Mary Immaculate for the people of God.

It is not enough to defend ourselves only, but we must also gain conquests for the Blessed Virgin. For you by your kindness, by your humility, by your exactitude in frequenting the sacraments and in fulfilling your duties of state, especially by a Christian union, you will cause others with whom you meet to understand how sweet it is to belong entirely to Mary.

True missionaries ought never to count on themselves, on their talents or their industry, but they ought to put all their confidence in the help of grace and their mission, and also in the protection of the Blessed Virgin, who is laboring at this work for which she was elevated to the Divine Maternity.

The true secret of success in any work, whether it be for one's own perfection or for the support of religion and the propagation of the Faith, it is to interest the Blessed Virgin in it, to refer all the glory of it to her, according to the views and sentiments of our Lord Jesus Christ.

Once you have become practically the slave of the good Lord, the very special son and missionary of the Blessed Virgin, you will participate abundantly in the liberty of the children of God, and you will experience with delight all the precious effects of the consecration of your entire being to His service.

Be truly faithful to the Lord, not as a slave, because of fear, but as a good son, because of love. Penetrate yourself often with the thought of all that He has done and suffered for you, and of all the graces that He grants you. May He always reign in you, may you love to depend entirely on Him and to do nothing except for Him and His Virgin Mother, especially during your prayers, meditations, and Holy Communions.

CHAPTER THREE

Mystical Body of Christ

Father Chaminade's conviction on the best means of fulfilling the New Testament of Christ is to study and expose the most sublime and most beautiful doctrines of St. John and St. Paul on the life of grace. The life of grace is best understood by us mortals through understanding of the doctrine of the Mystical Body of Christ. It is the principal theme in the Pauline epistle and fundamental doctrine in the spirituality of Father Chaminade. With this doctrine of the Mystical Body as outlined by St. Paul and the Divine Maternity as taught in the Gospel, we have a foundation, claims Father Chaminade, to become truly alter Christus (another Christ), the object of true glorification of God, the final end of all human creatures.

I. THE HEAD AND THE MEMBERS

Because Jesus Christ is our Head we must have an essential and eternal dependence on Him; we must always live by His Spirit and share His life, we must always act by His order and inspiration and always open our hearts to His divine influence.

As the head holds the highest rank in the natural body and as it is from there that the soul animates the whole body, so also Jesus Christ has the highest rank in His Mystical Body. It is from Him that all the members receive life and holiness.

As the head is intimately united with the body, so Jesus Christ is intimately united to the body of His Church from which He can never separate Himself. All bodies and all societies that do not have Jesus Christ as head are not His body, because He is not united to them and because He does not govern them by the influence of His Spirit.

The grace of Redemption, which is applied to us in Holy Baptism, makes us the property of God to such an extent as to make us partakers of the Divine Nature by associating us with the life of the God-Man so that we are with Him one and the same Christ. Consequently, this grace of Baptism consecrates us forever as members of Jesus Christ and temples of the Holy Spirit so that as children of the Church we become the fullness of His body.

There are several wonderful effects of this divine life with which the Mystical Body is animated:

As the effect of grace is to heal our sick nature, it heals our will which sin had impaired and it also heals our intellect which was no less obscured, so that by the one, man should know what he ought to do and by the other what he would be able to do . . . grace is an unction, an oil, that cures and illumines.

God is not only where you are, but He is in you in the very core of your soul. He enlivens it, He animates it, and He sustains it by His divine presence. For as the soul, which is present in the whole body, nevertheless as it is frequently spoken of as residing in the heart in a special manner, so God who is present in all things is much more so in our soul. It is this that St. Paul means when he says that we live, that we move, that we are in God.

It is grace by which God gives us that by which we can accomplish what He has ordered. It is what He promised in very many places in Scripture. Shall we doubt His fidelity or the power of His grace? It is God Himself who accomplishes in us what He demands of us.

Sin is the privation of all (supernatural) good and the source of all evil. It deprives us of grace which is the life of our soul and of all the supernatural good that accompanies it. It carries off Charity and the cardinal virtues and the seven gifts of the Holy Spirit. It deprives us of all the merit of our good works and of all the rights that we have acquired in heaven. It troubles the peace of our consciences and deprives us of the caresses and consolations of the Holy Spirit. Finally it causes us to lose God.

The state of mortal sin is therefore a state of death. It is the spiritual death of the soul in this sense that it deprives it of grace and the Spirit of God which is the life of the soul.

Sinners are both the executioners and the cross of the Son of God, for in renewing the cause of His suffering and death, they endeavor with all their power to crucify Him anew; and as the members of a Christian are the members of Jesus Christ, it is really Jesus Christ who is as it were crucified in them.

By sin Jesus Christ is tied up and rendered helpless to act in us. For example, our avarice nails down His charity; our anger, His meekness; our impatience, His patience; our pride, His humility; and so by our vices we find, we flay, and we cut to pieces Jesus Christ dwelling in us.

Finally, the sinner who believes, remains nevertheless united to Jesus Christ as a member of the Mystical Body, but as a paralyzed member. Venial sin, on the other hand, does not drive the Holy Spirit from our hearts, but it sorrows and afflicts Him. The Holy Spirit is then in our hearts in inexpressible sorrow. Habitual imperfections, be they ever so small, are more dangerous to the divine union and to progress in virtue than the greatest of sins of surprise.

The union of Christ with the members is only obtained by membership in the Church, for: (a) Outside of this chaste spouse there is no union with the groom. She alone has the advantages of this divine union, and she alone has received the keys which are a mark of the power attached to the union. She alone is united to the groom, and she alone possesses the fecundity which is the fruit of this union. (b) There is no life outside the Church, because all the life which can be had can come only from her. And no one possesses this life unless he belongs to her. (c) Outside of the Church there is no salvation.

The Mystical Body of Christ is not a metaphysical, but a real, union — a union more perfect than that of the human body.

It is a union by which all the living members of the Church share whatever they have and by which the riches, strength, and health of one becomes by charity the (supernatural) riches, strength, and health of another. It is a union by which all the living parts of the body of the Church are truly noble, if not in themselves, then at least in the union which they have with the whole body. It is also a union which makes the living members of the Church not only members of Jesus Christ, but in a very true sense, Jesus Christ Himself.

By Baptism Jesus Christ takes a true possession of the Christian in order to communicate that life to him which His Holy Humanity receives from the divinity by His Hypostatic Union. But note well that the baptized receives the divine life only by communication and that he remains always free, that his union with Jesus Christ, although very true, is but a moral union, for which our Lord shows the necessity in these few words: "Without Me you are able to do nothing."

The depth of God's love is expressed in the union of His divine nature with human nature, the union in which His eternal Word is as it were hidden behind the face of human nature. The depth of Christ's love is expressed in the union of His divine humanity with the members of His Church, a union so intimate that Jesus Christ lives in His members. By the first union, God and man are but one in Jesus Christ. It can be said that by the second, the Man-God and the Christian are but one. Between God and the Man-God all things are in common. So between the Man-God and the Christian all things are in common.

Hence, our union with Christ gives rise to certain duties and special benefits. They are: (a) the duty of a continual dependence on this divine head so that our whole conduct follows only the movements and impressions of His Spirit and that we will only what is in accord with His divine will; (b) the duty of repeated interior acts which will strengthen this union and accustom us to pray, act, and suffer in union with the prayers, actions, and sufferings of Jesus Christ: (c) the duty of doing and suffering all that we can in order to preserve the union of all the members and never to break it.

By Him and with Him and in Him, to use the phrase from the Canon of the Mass, we can reflect on the duties as outlined above. To act by Jesus Christ is to make oneself entirely dependent on His Spirit and His grace — on His Spirit by doing everything that He orders, and on His grace by recognizing that we can do nothing without His help. To act with Jesus Christ is to seek to imitate in this action the virtue which is applicable to it. To act in Jesus Christ is to unite oneself to Him in such a way as to be one with Him; it is to act as a member of a body of which He is the Head.

II. THE SPIRIT OF CHRIST IN THE MYSTICAL BODY

The "Spirit of Christ" is a term frequently used by Father Chaminade when making applications of our life in the Mystical Body of Christ. It is well to note that Pope Pius XII also used the term in his encyclical on the Mystical Body of Christ. Saint-Jure in his book L'Homme Spirituel (Paris: R. Ruffet, 1863, pp. 34–36) lists five different meanings to the term.

"The Spirit of Jesus Christ can be understood in two ways, in itself and in us. Considered in itself, this Spirit is first of all His divinity, or, if you like, His divine Person; for God is Spirit. Secondly, this Spirit is the Holy Spirit, the third Person of the Most Holy and August Trinity; because He proceeds from Him (Christ) as well as from the Father. Finally, the Spirit of Jesus Christ, still considered in itself, is all the operations of the divinity of Jesus, both towards itself and towards His humanity, and reciprocally, all the operations of His humanity towards His divinity; in a word, it is the whole divine life of this admirable compound, of this God-man; the manner in which He knew, in which He esteemed, in which He honored and loved God; the manner in which He thought, spoke, and put into operation all His spiritual and corporal faculties. But if we consider the Spirit of Jesus Christ in ourselves, it is the Holy Spirit who is called the Spirit of Jesus, because Jesus has merited Him for us and because it is in virtue of His merits that this Spirit comes into us to dwell, to fortify us with His hope, to urge us continually to embrace His (Christ's) doctrine and to imitate His life. This Spirit of Jesus Christ is also the participation and resemblance that we have with Him (Christ) and with His manner of thinking and acting."

Of these terms, Father Chaminade rarely used the first, but the others he used interchangeably and even equivalently.

The spiritual life is the very life of Jesus Christ. St. Paul expresses it: "It is now no longer I that live, but Christ lives in me" (Gal. 2:20). A true Christian is another Jesus Christ. The spirit of Jesus Christ, the life of Jesus Christ is the manner of life that Jesus Christ observed. And the principle that sustained Jesus Christ and that acted in Him to lead Him to follow this manner of life is the Holy Spirit who inspired in Him this way of life.

Adapting St. Augustine's words, we may say: Christ gives life to all the members, He sees by their eyes, He hears by their ears, He speaks by their tongues, He works with their hands, He walks with their feet, He is in all the members to give them life and in giving life to all, He makes it possible for each one to accomplish his mission.

This great union is formed by the Holy Spirit which Jesus Christ has received in all its plenitude and which He communicates to all His members according to the measure proper to them. This Spirit is, as it were, the soul of this great body, by which it lives and is animated. There are not two spirits in this body. The same Spirit which is in the Head is also in the Body and in each member in particular. "For in one Spirit," says St. Paul, "we were all baptized into one body, whether Jews or Gentiles, whether slaves or free; and we were all given to drink of one Spirit" (1 Cor. 12:13).

St. Paul felt within himself two men, as it were, one of which wished only good, the other only evil. It is the same in us. Why? Because in us there are two principles of life, one of the supernatural life and the other of sin, of concupiscence. As Christians it is the Holy Spirit who is our principle of life and who awakens in us the desire for virtue. But there is also concupiscence, the principle of evil, which leads us to sin. Hence the battle. What the Spirit wishes, the flesh does not and vice versa. As a result the Spirit must fight against the flesh, otherwise we shall die.

To live is to have an interior principle of movement. To live spiritually is to have no other interior principle of movement than the Holy Spirit, to act only by the Spirit of Jesus Christ, to live

only His Spirit, and to cease all other movements. To live according to the flesh is to have as interior principle of one's thoughts
and actions the inspirations of the flesh or of corrupted nature.

Can it be said that he who does not give in to his passions
and vices, who commits no great sins, who mortifies himself even
in certain things, lives a spiritual life? No. The spiritual life is
the very life of Jesus Christ. St. Paul expresses it: "It is now no
longer I that live, but Christ lives in me" (Gal. 2:20).

That which is called life is an interior principle of movement.
It is the Holy Spirit who dwells in us. The Spirit of God enlightens
us just as He did Jesus Christ. St. Paul says: "Have this mind
in you which was also in Christ Jesus" (Phil. 2:5). If you live the
life of Christ you will see as He does, think, feel, love, and judge
as He does.

By the term "desires of the flesh" St. Paul understands every
kind of vice. In the epistle to the Galatians (5:19–22) he enumer-
ates the vices of the flesh. They are vices of the soul rather than
the body, but they have come to us by the body. Our subject is
not to distinguish between these vices but to consider what life
we are to lead. The desires of the flesh are not the vices of impurity.
They are all vice.

It seems important to me that we understand what is the "old
man" and, on the other hand, what is the "new man," the regenerated man; how Jesus Christ is mystically crucified by the sinner
and how Christians filled with the Spirit of Jesus Christ crucify in
themselves the old man. For a proper understanding of these
profound truths we must take into consideration both the three
evil inclinations which make up the life of sin or of "the old man"
and the three contrary inclinations which are effected in Christians
by the Spirit of Jesus Christ. These inclinations of the Christian
are, as it were, three mystical nails which attach the old man to
the cross.

Religious and all Christians alike should live the life of the
Spirit of Jesus, that is, of Jesus Crucified. To this end they must:
(1) go out of themselves; (2) rise above themselves; (3) do
violence to themselves.

Finally, here are the three principal characteristics of the Spirit of God or the characteristics of the Christian:

a) The spirit of separation, of recollection, and of prayer by opposition to the worldly spirit of dissipation. It is an entirely interior life opposed to an exterior one.

b) The spirit of renouncement and of penance which is opposed to the spirit of laziness and immortification and of indulgence in all our disorderly penchants.

c) The spirit of strength and courage, which is opposed to the submissive and conformist spirit.

III. SACRAMENTS OF THE MYSTICAL BODY

Although all seven Sacraments are similar to the arteries and veins that circulate life-giving blood to all members of the body, yet Father Chaminade recognizes three Sacraments in particular that activate the members to life, to strength, and to union. They are the Sacraments of Baptism, Confirmation, and Holy Eucharist.

This wonderful union of the Mystical Body of Christ is formed by the Sacraments which are, as it were, the veins, the channels which carry the blood, the Spirit, and the life of Jesus Christ to all members to enable them to carry out their individual functions.

It is faith that prepares the subject to be grafted. And in what does the graft itself consist? Among Christians it is the Sacrament of Baptism. And after the graft, what is necessary? Is it not necessary that the graft grow firm and be strengthened? This is achieved by Confirmation. And after that what must be done? Once this life is possessed, it must be maintained by the Eucharist.

But as a business that makes large profits, they receive the largest share who have invested the greatest sum. In the same way Jesus Christ, who is the Head, the Bond, the Master of this spiritual concern, distributes its goods and profits according to the merits of each one. These merits and profits, however, are the gifts of Jesus Christ, who by His death and His other mysteries gives them their force and their value. Thus in this concern, everything depends upon union with the Head.

Unless a man be born again of water and the Spirit, he cannot enter the kingdom of God. The expression "born again" supposes that man had first of all received the supernatural being, but that he had lost it or that he had destroyed it. Our Savior here opposes supernatural generation to carnal generation which cannot be repeated. By the latter we are born "children of wrath"; by the former, so necessary, children of God and Christians. As in the generation of the flesh, this supernatural generation is accomplished by two principles, water and the Holy Spirit.

First, to die unceasingly to sin. It is true that by Baptism sin is made to die in me, that is, in my soul which was sullied and which grace has purified. But not in my body, in my flesh which is still corrupted and which unceasingly revolts against the spirit. Now, it is to this disorder of nature that I must die continually. It is the obligation which Baptism imposes on me. The views of Jesus Christ ought to be as so many nails with which I crucify the contrary views of fallen nature: thus, by humility I will nail down pride, etc.

As a second promise that is made in Baptism, we live the life of grace. "Alive to God," that is, in the state of grace. Alive for God, that is, glorifying Him by our conduct, continually advancing in perfection.

With the grace of Baptism we receive the Holy Spirit to form us in the quality of the spiritual infancy of Jesus Christ or, in the words of St. Peter, "as newborn babes." It is the grace of Baptism which by the operation of the Holy Spirit brings us into spiritual conformity with the state of the Holy Infancy of Jesus Christ.

Because Baptism is a Sacrament of the New Law, it produces what it represents and signifies, so that at the same time that it represents in us the mysteries of the death and resurrection of Jesus Christ, it at the same time produces the effects of these mysteries.

This Sacrament produces two principal effects, namely, death and life. We can distinguish death to sin and the new life according to which we must conduct ourselves.

Baptism is a spiritual death. Baptism is a spiritual resurrection. First, a spiritual death, because we have been buried in water to die with Jesus Christ. "For we were buried with him by means of

Baptism unto death." Second, a spiritual resurrection, because after having been buried under the water we come out of it again as from our tomb in order to live a new life, just as Jesus Christ, after having been buried, rose again for the glory of His Father and lived a new life. "As Christ has risen from the dead through the glory of the Father, so we also may walk in newness of life."

Jesus Christ, who abides in us by faith, has purified and sanctified us by Baptism and has withdrawn us from sin, which still exists in our nature. Jesus Christ Himself communicates to souls grand and noble sentiments, and a soul, thus united to Christ, finds herself in continual conflict with nature, which was not regenerated as she was. Hence, the incessant struggle between the flesh and the Spirit of which St. Paul speaks. Yet we will arrive at the complete shedding of the old man only upon our entrance into heaven.

The grace of Confirmation is like a solid food that by the proportioned operation of the Holy Spirit makes us grow spiritually in Jesus Christ to the age of maturity. For this reason it is said that Confirmation renders us perfect Christians. . . . In order to arouse this precious grace, it is necessary to do in a spirit of penance what one should have done in order to receive this Sacrament: (a) instruct oneself on what regards the Sacrament of Confirmation; (b) purify more and more one's conscience; (c) increase the desires for this Sacrament by multiplying acts; (d) pray and invoke the Holy Spirit.

The action of the Holy Spirit is represented in the ceremony of the sacrament by the imposition of hands. It signifies that he is chosen by God in special way and that he ought to be led and directed by the hand, as it were, as one of his children who has received a more abundant participation in the spirit of adoption.

The effects of Confirmation are a grace and a character which render us perfect Christians and soldiers of Jesus Christ. It is by this Sacrament that the Holy Spirit purges, cleans, sanctifies, perfects, and consecrates a soul so nobly that He puts it, by His divine and secret operations, in the immediate disposition for receiving the Sacred Body of Jesus Christ. Confirmation renders a soul strong and generous so that it can support its cross and all kinds of adversity.

By the worthy reception of His natural body, we become the members of His Mystical Body in a more excellent manner than by any other Sacrament. It is particularly by Communion that the Lord makes reign this Spirit in our hearts. The Eucharist is the extension of the Incarnation.

This is the proper effect of the Sacrament wherein man becomes not only of one mind with Jesus Christ, but, in a way, even of one body. According to the Apostle, "Because the bread is one, we, though many, are one body, all of us who partake of the one bread." (a) Union according to the spirit: "He who cleaves to the Lord is one spirit with Him." (b) Union according to the flesh: "Because we are members of his body, made from his flesh and his bones." We can say then: "It is now no longer I that live, but Christ lives in me." We are incorporated in Christ. This incorporation, according to St. Paul, begins with Baptism: "We were all baptized into one body," and is consummated by the Eucharist: "He who eats my flesh and drinks my blood, abides in me and I in him."

It is principally by Holy Communion that this Spirit of union begins to reign in our hearts. For just as our soul begins to animate the food which we consume at the moment it is united to the body, so the Spirit who animates the humanity of the Savior and who is, as it were, the soul of His soul, begins to animate us as soon as we become His members by Communion. And just as our natural spirit emanates from the head into the whole body to give it movement and life, so in the Mystical Body of Christ, the Holy Spirit descends from the Head to all the faithful who are His members to give them divine life.

We have the honorable obligation to hear Mass because we are the mystical members of Jesus Christ and because we are all part of the victim immolated on the altar. You know that at the Holy Sacrifice of the Mass there are two kinds of victims, one interior and imperceptible, the other exterior and perceptible and the symbol of the former.

The perceptible victim is the Body and Blood of Jesus Christ hidden under the species of bread and wine. The interior and imperceptible victim is His Mystical Body; it is the Church composed of all the faithful. All Christians, says St. Augustine, are but one body and this body is the host of their sacrifice. The two bodies, mystical and natural, are, as it were, but two parts of the same victim. It follows then that whether we consider the perceptible Host or whether we consider the imperceptible one, it is solely the Son of God who is immolated to His Father in the sacrifice on our altars.

How are we to be victims with Jesus Christ? The exterior and bloody sacrifice is not the only one of which Jesus Christ is our model on Calvary. The interior sacrifice of submission, of obedience to His Father's will, has never been interrupted. The character of the perpetual sacrifice of Jesus is His perfect submission to the divine will. The first act of this sacrifice was to say to His Father on entering the world, "I come to do your will." The continuation of this sacrifice during His life was, as He Himself said, in doing whatever He willed. The consummation of this sacrifice was to say to God in accepting the chalice of His Passion, "Father, not my will but thine be done," and to be obedient to His death on the cross. The perpetuity of this sacrifice in heaven is to have but one will with His Father and on earth to go so far as to be dependent on creatures in order to reunite them all to Himself, if possible, in the perfect submission which is due the Sovereign Majesty of God. The sacrifice that He demands of His creatures, then, ought to be an interior one, as is His in the divine Eucharist. It ought to be more a sacrifice of their soul than their body, more the sacrifice of their natural inclinations and their earthly desires than their temporal good, more the sacrifice of their will always submissive to the divine will, always in complete conformity with the will of the Father as was Jesus Christ's.

There are six kinds of offerings we must make as part of the "royal priesthood" and our life should be a continuity of offerings which we are to make to God.

a) The sacrifice of adoration and praise of God which we make as the priests of inanimate creatures.

b) The sacrifice of detachment from all things considering ourselves only as voyagers on earth traveling toward our heavenly country.

c) The sacrifice of privation, denying ourselves all that faith forbids and condemns.

d) The sacrifice of expiation by our penances for past sins and for preservation from future ones.

e) The sacrifice of resignation, seeing the will of God in all things by our faith.

f) The sacrifice of abnegation, never seeking ourselves but only God and His good pleasure in all things.

This miracle ought to produce in us a similar one, namely, the separation of our evil inclinations and vices from our soul, to which, one might say, they are joined as if to their substance. The word of God operates the first miracle in the Blessed Sacrament every day on our altars. It also operates the second, which is the end of the first, if we are obedient and if we co-operate with the grace whose fullness is in the Blessed Sacrament.

Our Savior has continued after His death to procure for men this religion toward God by all the inventions of His love. . . . In order to dilate this holy religion toward God and to multiply it in our souls, He comes to us and leaves Himself on earth in the hands of priests as the Victim of praise in order to communicate His Spirit of the host. It is to this point of perfection to which He calls us in this life. By His intimate presence in us and by His living fire He consumes us. He communicates to us the most perfect state of His religion through the worthy reception of the Sacred Host.

PART TWO

Perfection and the Means to Attain It

> Oh, how I wish you to become a saint.
> Let the terms saint and child of Mary
> be synonymous.
>
> — Father Chaminade

CHAPTER ONE

Perfection

I. A BLUEPRINT FOR SANCTITY

Now having looked at God through His Son Jesus Christ in the Mystical Body and the Divine Maternity of the Blessed Virgin Mary, we may begin to look at ourselves and how we must live as members of the Mystical Body and sons of Mary. The fullest attainment of our life in Christ is called perfection and — when confirmed in heaven — sainthood. Father Chaminade frequently reminded his spiritual children that their first vocation in life is to become a saint. If anything less, it is not living for our final end. In this chapter we shall see the meaning of perfection, the method by which this perfection is sure to be obtained and the primary means of grace.

There are three ages in which, step by step, man would become once again the perfect man; in this world he would repair his innocence, in heaven he would gain peace, and at the general resurrection he would receive immortality. Thus he would arrive at that maturity which is proportioned to the completed growth of Christ.

But before man could avail himself of these three ages, there are three conclusions he must accept and fulfill. The first is that man accept the decree of death, and the humiliating consequences such as sickness, sufferings, vexations, fear, the rebellion of the passions, the sorrowful and deplorable effects of concupiscence, etc., which Christ did not revoke by His redemption. The second condition is that men hear His adorable Son, that they believe His word, that they take Him for their mediator, that they follow His example, that they observe His laws; that they incorporate themselves in Him so as to live only by Him and that they take advantage of His merits. The third condition is that God obliges Himself to return man not only to the rights of Adam in innocence, but to the rights of their mediator, Jesus Christ, so that if we accomplish the first two conditions, God will give us a share of the glory of Jesus Christ Himself.

Jesus Christ, who abides in us by faith, has purified and sanctified us by Baptism and has withdrawn us from sin, which still exists in our nature. Jesus Himself communicates to souls grand and noble sentiments, and a soul thus united to Christ finds herself in continual conflict with nature, which was not regenerated as she was. Hence the incessant struggle between the flesh and the Spirit of which St. Paul speaks.

Yet we will arrive at the complete shedding of the old man only upon our entrance into heaven.

Understand that the old man has been crucified in Jesus Christ in order that the body of sin be destroyed and we commit it no more. In order to properly understand this text, we must know: (a) that in every sacrifice we can distinguish an interior one and an exterior one — the exterior one is the sensible victim that is immolated and destroyed, and the interior one is the oblation of self to God by which one recognizes the sovereign domain of God over all creatures; (b) that by the old man is meant depraved nature, passion, concupiscence, and the inclination to evil. Now the death of Jesus properly signifies our old man. Such is the interpretation of "the death of Christ signifies the interior death of our nature." With the above explanations, this text is easily understood. The exterior sacrifice of Jesus is our old man, and this old man, which is the body of sin, has been sacrificed at the same time as Jesus Christ, that is, at the same time that Jesus Christ is immolated internally with the old man. Jesus Christ has immolated this old man in order that the body of sin be destroyed, that is, that concupiscence and our inclination to evil be conquered by the grace which He has merited and which does not allow us to sin again.

It is only by Jesus Christ that we are reconciled to God, that we render Him a cult worthy of His infinite grandeur, that we are made His heirs, that grace is given to us, that the gates of heaven are opened to us. The Christian religion is entirely founded on Jesus Christ. All the worship and all the honor that it renders to God, all the doctrine that it teaches, all the rules that it prescribes, all the promises that it makes, all the hopes that it gives, have their source in Jesus Christ.

We must render to God a great number of religious duties that we are unable to render Him by ourselves, as to adore Him, to love Him, to praise Him, to petition Him as we ought and as He deserves. Jesus Christ by His charity accomplishes our duties by proxy, as it were, and so becomes the Mediator of our religion. For that reason He wished to rise again after His death and be always living, says St. Paul, that is, to praise and petition His Father in our place and because of our inability.

We must not, however, speak so much of this mystic death to the world and to self that we lose sight of the precious life in Christ which should follow it. We die only to live. The whole of Christianity, the whole of perfection consists of this death and of this life. It is the doctrine of St. Paul. Think of yourselves as dead to sin, and alive with a life that looks toward God, through Christ Jesus our Lord.

But it is not only death that Jesus Christ gives to His disciples. If He wishes that they die to the world, it is to make them live His life and to transform them into other Christs.

Christianity embraces a plan of perfection so high and so divine that the life of God must serve as its model.

What is this object? The most sublime perfection of man in this life is to be united to God in such a manner, that his soul, centered in God, with all its faculties and all its powers, becomes one spirit with Him, so much so that he remembers only God, and that he thinks only of God, that he relishes nothing but God, and that all his affections mingled with transports of divine love, bear sweetly upon the sole enjoyment of his Creator. For the image of God is impressed on the three faculties of the soul, i.e., on the understanding, the memory, and the will; and as long as the image of God is not wholly impressed on the soul, the latter is not Godlike;

for God is the form which must be impressed upon the soul like a seal upon wax (cf. St. Bonaventure). Now this impression is never perfect, if the intelligence is not fully enlightened, within its capacity, by the knowledge of God who is the Supreme Truth; if the will is not perfectly moved by the love of the Sovereign Good, and if the memory is not completely absorbed by the prospect and continual remembrance of Happiness Itself.

This perfection consists in submitting one's reason to the sovereign reason of God, in renouncing one's own views, one's own will, all the natural inclinations of self-love and this on account of that self-disdain which the Son of God recommends so much in His Gospel to those who would be His disciples.

Perfection consists in putting off the old man and putting on the new. Now, what is the old man? It is our corrupt nature, which we have received from our first father as an inheritance. This nature must be annihilated, and put off entirely to make room for the new Adam, that is Jesus Christ.

The old Adam is earthly, being formed of earth; the new Adam is heavenly, having come down from His heavenly home. The former seeks only the things that satisfy nature, the latter is happy when deprived of these satisfactions. The one looks for the esteem of creatures, the other desires naught but their contempt. The former toils for transitory things and clings to the earth, the latter despises all earthly things, rising unceasingly to things eternal, to his heavenly home, to God his Father.

The word "perfection" is easily uttered; its full import, however, is greater than we think. To speak of anyone being perfect means to say that he loves and serves God perfectly, but to love God perfectly means to love Him with our whole heart, our whole mind, and our whole strength.

We love God with our whole heart, when all the love that our heart is capable of is consecrated to Him. If we be allowed to love anything besides, in accordance with justice, reason, and the will of God, that affection, however just and reasonable, must be subordinated to the love we owe God who, in our hearts, must have the preference over everything else.

We love God with our whole mind if our mind is habitually

occupied with this thought and if He is the Origin, the Object, and the Supreme End of all our thoughts.

We love God with our whole soul when all the faculties of our soul are consecrated to Him and when we make use of them only to make Him known, loved, and served.

Finally, we love God with our whole strength when we display this strength in the same manner as stated above and consecrate, undividedly, unreservedly, and unrelentingly to His service, our life, our health, and all that we have and are.

May the thought of that perfection which God desires of us stimulate our courage and faith. In the morning upon awakening, far from giving way to our natural levity, let us say to ourselves: "O my soul, consider your work of this day; God calls you to perfection; through His intimate union with you He wishes to make you a participant of His divinity. What an honor and what a glory! O my God, I shall hasten and I resolve to employ well this new day which you are about to grant me."

The Apostle St. Paul tells us in these words: "The Lord chose us that we should be holy and unspotted in his sight" (Eph. 1:4).

a) Be holy. If the Lord has chosen us to be consecrated to Him in a special manner, to be His aids, His servants, His ambassadors, His chosen children, to whom, if not to us, has He given this precept: "Be ye holy, as your heavenly Father is holy."

b) Be unspotted. What is it to be a saint? It is to practice every virtue. God, however, asks even more of us. He desires that we be unsullied by any imperfection; that we be irreproachable; that by the integrity of our virtue we overcome the world; that we oblige the world to respect in us God and His holy law; that our good example confound the malevolent and put a stop to the prejudice of ignorance and inconsiderateness. As St. Peter says: "That by doing well, you may put to silence the ignorance of foolish men" (1 Peter 2:15). Finally, God desires that we may be able to say to His enemies what the Apostles told them, "examine us well; we have injured no man; nor have we corrupted anyone." Be as sinless as the divine Master who said to the Jews, "Who of you shall convince me of sin?"

The path of perfection is indeed narrow and difficult for the worldly-minded only; the servants of God find it broad and comfortable. And wherein lies the reason of this difference, of the contradictory views, if not in the difference of the dispositions to be found in the former and latter? The yoke of the Lord is sweet if we take it upon ourselves generously and bear it with constancy.

The path of perfection is not so well frequented as the way of the Commandments, but it is far more safe. The servant who does merely what the master demands of him is less worthy, and has less assurance of his master's protection in time of need, than the one who not only obeys, but even anticipates the very wishes of his master. Let us devote ourselves to the service with our whole hearts and God will be with us and for us.

Our perfection, as God understands it, does not consist in doing many or extraordinary things. The perfection to which God calls us depends on the care with which we perform our most ordinary actions. To perform all our actions well we must be exact, fervent, and persevering. We must also perform them with the interior spirit and be actuated by a principle of religion. This religious principle will be the soul and life of our actions.

If you were more fervent and more prudent, you would make use of every means to advance in virtue. If you could but attain the virtue and the perfection to which you are called, every year of your life would be a happy one and the eternity to follow unspeakably so. But the attainment of perfection as well as our work of saving souls are ends that cannot be accomplished without the special protection of the Blessed Virgin.

II. A METHOD OF GAINING SANCTITY

For gaining perfection, Father Chaminade, after twenty-five years of spiritual direction of religious and nonreligious, drew up a map of spiritual growth. The plan has been called by several names; however, the System of Virtues seems to be the most descriptive. By this systematic method of gaining virtue, Father Chaminade hoped to make perfect men, that is, saints and true children of Mary. He began with the concept of perfection as stated by St. Paul: "putting off the Old Man and putting on the New Man."

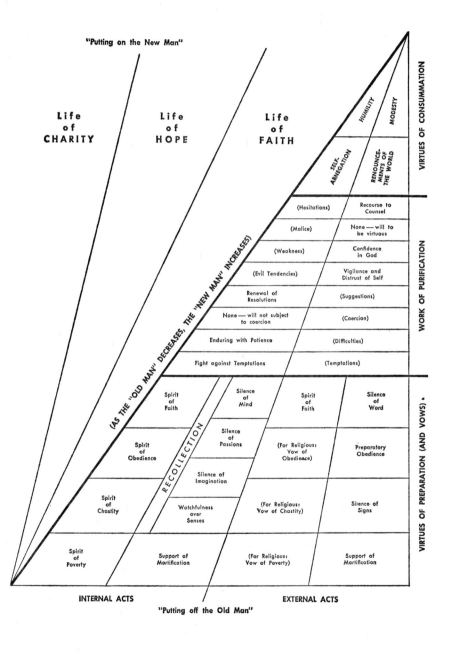

"Putting on the New Man"

Life of CHARITY   Life of HOPE   Life of FAITH

HUMILITY   MODESTY

SELF-ABNEGATION   RENOUNCE-MENTS OF THE WORLD

VIRTUES OF CONSUMMATION

(Hesitations) — Recourse to Counsel

(Malice) — None — will to be virtuous

(Weakness) — Confidence in God

(Evil Tendencies) — Vigilance and Distrust of Self

Renewal of Resolutions — (Suggestions)

None — will not subject to coercion — (Coercion)

Enduring with Patience — (Difficulties)

Fight against Temptations — (Temptations)

WORK OF PURIFICATION

(AS THE "OLD MAN" DECREASES, THE "NEW MAN" INCREASES)

Spirit of Faith   Silence of Mind   Spirit of Faith   Silence of Word

Spirit of Obedience   Silence of Passions   (For Religious: Vow of Obedience)   Preparatory Obedience

RECOLLECTION

Silence of Imagination

Spirit of Chastity   Watchfulness over Senses   (For Religious: Vow of Chastity)   Silence of Signs

Spirit of Poverty   Support of Mortification   (For Religious: Vow of Poverty)   Support of Mortification

VIRTUES OF PREPARATION (AND VOWS)

INTERNAL ACTS   EXTERNAL ACTS

"Putting off the Old Man"

Some years ago, a disciple of Father Chaminade drew up in a diagram the whole System of Virtues. The author of the diagram, Very Reverend Father William Ferree, S.M., Ph.D., became Second Assistant to the Superior General of the Society of Mary in 1956. With his permission we reproduce that diagram. As the reader advances through the remainder of this chapter it will be advisable to refer back to this diagram for a clearer understanding of the System of Virtues.

Father Chaminade developed the system into four degrees. They were: Virtues of Preparation, Purification, Consummation, and lastly the full life of faith in the presence of God. Some may ask what is the comparison between his system and that of the traditional way of perfection. Seemingly the two systems permit no comparison, although the two systems do overlap, yet the System of Virtues is presumed well advanced by the time the soul ventures into the illuminative way and the unitive way. Thus the purgative way and the System of Virtues overlap particularly in the objective. The System of Virtues is intended as a means of progressing in the ways of spiritual perfection.

Father Chaminade, in one of his most valuable writings, known as Premier Jet des Exercises outlines the steps toward perfection. It is believed that he wrote it about 1830; however, we know that he taught the method as early as 1816. He was never entirely satisfied with the outline and often attempted to improve it. This outline is the last known attempt directly authored by himself. It is upon the 1830 edition that we base the following sections of the chapter.

The first system of virtues for perfection:

I. Virtues of Preparation

    A. SILENCE (the word is used to mean constant and deliberate control)
        1. Exterior silence: words and signs
        2. Interior silence: spirit, imagination, passions

B. RECOLLECTION
  1. In prayer
  2. While studying and reading
  3. At work and recreation
C. OBEDIENCE
  1. Prompt
  2. Entire
D. SUPPORT OF MORTIFICATIONS
  1. Interior difficulties
  2. Exterior difficulties
  3. Trials
  4. Penances
  5. Reproaches

(By the practice of these virtues one is disposed to enter into the way of perfection.)

II. **Virtues of Purification**
  A. THOSE THAT PURIFY THE SOUL BY THE STRENGTH OF FAITH
    1. Interior obstacles — by faith
    2. Evil inclinations — by virtuous inclinations
    3. Hesitations or incertitude of conduct — by the opening of the soul and recourse to counsel
  B. THOSE WHICH PRECAUTION THE SOUL AGAINST EXTERIOR OBSTACLES
    1. Contrarieties — by enduring patience
    2. Suggestions of the worldly-minded by maxims of the Gospel and renewal of resolutions
    3. Temptations of the devil by a spiritual combat and flight

III. **Virtues of Consummation**
  A. HUMILITY — not to regard self as the end
  B. INTERIOR MODESTY — no intrusion of self into the apostolate
  C. SELF-ABNEGATION — no "exploiting" of the apostolate for prestige, power, etc.
  D. RENOUNCEMENTS OF CREATURES — not to regard world or material things as an end

IV. All these Virtues of Preparation, Purification, and Consummation are indicated by the text of St. Peter, "Advance from faith to virtue, from virtue to knowledge, from knowledge to abstinence, from abstinence to patience, from patience to piety, from piety to fraternal love, from faternal love to divine charity" (2 Peter 1:6). The practice of these virtues will bring us to the knowledge of Jesus Christ and eternal life. Amen.

V. [In a quick stroke of the pen, Father Chaminade indicates what positive virtues should fill the void left by the negative action of the Preparation, Purification and Consummation.] We add to these Virtues of Consummation some reflections on the interior life that a good Son of Mary should lead: they are the life of faith, hope, and charity.

VI. Let us not forget to excite ourselves to the love of the Most Blessed and Immaculate Virgin Mary. We ought above all to imitate our Lord in this important point. It is by her maternal attentions that we become conformed to this divine Model. Let us allow ourselves to be directed by this tender Mother, our august Patron, and let us submit ourselves with joy to her direction. It is by this manner in particular that we bear witness to our love, our gratitude and our devotion to her.

Unfortunately, Father Chaminade made little progress in developing the outline he had so painstakingly composed. He had hoped to write a spiritual direction manual from the outline to be used by novice masters, superiors of religious orders, and confessors. He was over seventy when he began the manual, however administrative problems in the Society of Mary occupied the remainder of his life.

We have only extracts from the conferences on the subject of the virtues which his spiritual sons and daughters preserved for us. These extracts will constitute the last part of this chapter and will in some distant way echo what Father Chaminade would have written himself. It is also known that he was not entirely satisfied with the outline, for he felt certain areas needed more details. But he hoped to correct that when he wrote out his manual on direction.

Father Chaminade had, however, given the method to be used in obtaining the goal of these virtues. For him, silence meant willful control. He suggested that the beginner spend about a week on each of the preparatory virtues, using his meditations, spiritual examens, and reading to concentrate on the virtue of the week. The following week, the individual should take the next "silence" until all had been covered. By limiting the time rather than perfecting one virtue at a time he believed the beginner would not fall to discouragement. On the second time around on the virtues a longer time should be employed for each. After a year or so the individual should have mastered them sufficiently to concentrate a whole month on one virtue. However when the individual and the spiritual adviser felt that the necessary mastery had been accomplished this individual should move on to the next Virtues of Purification, there to repeat the process once more.

It matters little that some may object to calling these dispositions, these habits, virtues. By whatever name they are called, they are virtues for us. The general character of each is that it acts over and over again, and sustains itself by a willing relish, without altering peace of soul, and most of the time showing the natural signs of interior joy.

Let us conclude this preliminary exposition by saying: "Unless the Lord build the house, they labor in vain who build it" (Ps. 126:1). We outline methods because God wants our sanctification to be partly our work; and it is the characteristic note of our weakness that to do well whatever we do, we must proceed with order taking one thing after another; first, that which is more to our capacity, in order to get to what is beyond; but we realize at the same time that since this great work is also the work of God, we work in vain if He does not aid us with His powerful grace. We, therefore, beg it of Him with persevering insistence and humility. Our confidence lies in this, that it is he himself who calls us in these ways for his greater glory and our salvation.

These virtues teach us to know ourselves; show us how the soul prepares itself, becomes capable of examining itself. These virtues are called virtues of preparation because they facilitate self-knowledge.

I. Virtues of Preparation

A. EXTERIOR SILENCES
1. Silence of words

Silence of words consists in refraining from all speech. But as a religious virtue and according to the end of our work, we do not take silence in such an absolute manner. Our silence consists in never speaking without necessity and without utility to others. It is expressed in this short maxim: "To speak only when we wish and to wish only when it is necessary."

But isn't it a fact that one never speaks without wishing to? No, this is not true. How many times does not the tongue make us commit indiscretions that we are truly angry at afterward? How often in moments of lively discussion offensive words escape us that we repent afterward. Oh, if we never spoke except when we wished it, how many times we would be spared repentance for these offenses.

In effect, if we never speak except when we wish to do so, there will be nothing said by light-mindedness, indiscretion, or natural inclination. And if we speak only when we must, it will be only when necessity or charity makes it a duty. The practice of this virtue conceived in this manner is certainly more difficult than the observance of absolute silence. It demands a great attention to oneself and a true love of silence.

2. Silence of signs

We call signs all the exterior movements by which we express our thoughts and our sentiments as well as the manner in which we perform our actions. Two kinds of signs are therefore to be distinguished: those which express our thoughts and our sentiments; those that pertain to the actions and habits of our body.

By the word "sentiments" we primarily mean those various manifestations of our passions, so that this silence consists in the exterior regulation of our passions. The first are ordinarily named gestures. They accompany the voice and sometimes supply for it. It is the same for the passions; each passion manifests itself by particular gestures. The infinite variety of ways in which our thoughts can express themselves makes it impossible to offer any specific rules on their control. For the passions we can determine the signs which accompany them and which are the exterior manifestations of our heart.

We are ordered to silence the signs of our unworthy emotions so that bad example does not aggravate our fault; and we must silence our laudable emotions in order to keep them under the control of humility. Suppose that I feel a repugnance for a person. If she perceives by my signs this dislike, she might suffer greatly. Suppose I feel a great inconvenience in rendering a service and I allow this sentiment to be noticed by the others. It will injure her sensibility.

The silence of signs, then, consists in placing all movements under the control of the will in such a way as only to manifest what one wishes and that we suppress entirely what would be out of place in particular circumstances or even evil in itself. For this vigilance, courage of soul and oft-repeated acts are necessary. Our neighbor will draw from this virtue great edification; it will serve us as a great means toward taming the passions.

B. Interior Silences
1. Silence of spirit

When our words and signs are under control our spirit likes to speak with itself. It then recalls for us all which we already know. It forms and plans, joining to itself certain passions. As a consequence we can pass our whole life in dreams. All of our activity is consumed in things other than that proposed according to the place, time, and exercises demanded at the moment. It is a continual excursion outside of the object that is proposed for the object of reflection here and now. We go beyond the duty that is presently ours.

Thus we do less well what we are doing and we lose a good deal of time. Our spirit contracts a habit of light-mindedness and becomes ordinarily incapable of any sustained attention. We then carry even our distractions to our prayers and this holy exercise becomes sterile and painful. However, silence of spirit does not consist, as one might imagine, in suspending the action of our spirit as the silence of word restrained the action of the tongue. Our spirit cannot rest without thinking of something. Thus, silence of spirit is to fix our thoughts on that which should occupy it. In a word, to practice silence of spirit is to banish every useless thought in order to bring the spirit to the object which should occupy it.

If we do not take the necessary precaution our spirit will wander in a crowd of useless thoughts. This precaution consists in representing to oneself, at the beginning of the action, some object or some truth that is able to hold the spirit in the thoughts of piety.

Silence of spirit consists in stopping the continual wandering of our spirit. The means are: (a) to banish vain and useless thoughts and to occupy the spirit with something good and advantageous for the soul; to fix it on a subject and when we perceive that it has wandered, to bring it back to the subject; (b) to see if the unruliness of our spirit does not come from too great an attachment for an object; and (c) to examine if our useless thoughts are not a punishment of our curiosity and immortification of senses, our vanity, etc.

2. Silence of imagination

It gives to good the appearance of evil and to evil the appearance of good. The imagination creates chimeras and delivers our senses to them. The reason dominated by the imagination and by the senses rests ineffective, powerless.

It is an effect of the imagination that on occasions that offer little of peril, we believe ourselves in great danger and are driven on by fear. From this same source we are at times afflicted with great unhappiness which, in the eyes of others, is but a matter easy to support. On the other hand, one who is not dominated by his imagination sees each thing such as it really is and draws from events only those just conclusions dictated by reason.

The silence of imagination, therefore, consists in this: (a) We should examine if we have given way to reveries where our spirit entertains dangerous and illusory images. (b) We should examine if we have not exaggerated the sadnesses, joys, zeal, discouragement that befalls us. (c) We should examine if we have not acted often in consequence of our exaggerated thoughts in such a manner that when the moment of enthusiasm is passed we have repented for what we have said or done.

3. Silence of passions

The passion which ought to dominate in us, our only dominant passion in all our actions for all the circumstances of life, ought to be the love of God. However, often self-examination will show that some other motive has prompted us. An indication is accurately found by the pleasure or pain we experience in the act. According to St. John all that is not God can be traced either to the concupiscence of the eyes, the senses, or pride of life. Each one should examine which of these different passions dominates in him either habitually or occasionally. We must distinguish in our dominant passion that which influences us each day of our lives, and that which occurs only at certain times and in certain circumstances. Finally, in order to supplant unworthy passions with the love of God we must constantly work to destroy all the effects of the uncontrolled love which dominates us and then endeavor to fill our actions with the pure love of God.

Let us suppose that you perceive that you do most of your actions in order to be seen, esteemed, loved. It is then pride that is your dominant passion. If you see that all your actions are performed by vivacity of temperament and that the least thing excites you so that you are not able to speak tranquilly, it is then anger which is your dominant passion, etc.

We must take our faults of passion one by one, undertaking to correct that first of all which brings us to commit the most exterior faults and which might be the most dangerous for us. Thus St. Francis de Sales by this exercise arrived at the conquest of the anger which was his dominant passion and he thus became the gentlest of men. But it takes constancy and perseverance. This great saint needed more than twenty years to succeed.

With the five silences studied and practiced, the individual has advanced considerably on the road of the self-knowledge that will enable him to work more pointedly at the defects that must be overcome in order to allow the grace of God to work more freely.

Each one is to co-operate in the work of the silences to the best
of his ability and then advance to the next virtue of preparation,
returning to the silences at a later stage when the fuller development of grace will effect a deepening of the work begun in these
first days of the conversion to the life of perfection. It is nearly
impossible to possess all of the five silences in a perfect degree.
We ought simply to work at and acquire as perfectly as possible
what we can according to the grace which is given us. We should
have recognized by the study of the silences what is the faculty
which speaks most in us.

C. RECOLLECTION

This recollection is not the recollection which makes us absorbed in God, but the recollection consists in collecting and gather-
ing the efforts which have been proposed to us. We see where
we are, what is strong and what is weak. By recollection we understand ourselves and we have through it the means for remedying
the evils of the soul. Thus, if I see that I am weak on one point
and strong on another, I bring the strength to the aid of my
weakness and through knowledge that recollection has given me
I remedy the evil that might have made great progress.

I have said in examining the necessity of practicing silence for
each of our faculties, that the soul can be compared to an organ
recital where the pipes ought only to play according to the wish
of the musician and the plan of the piece. By the study of silence
we have recognized what pipes sound without a precise order and
which are solid and well ordered. Recollection in the most extended sense of the word is to hear no longer, to listen no more
to the indiscreet voices which arise in us against our will and our
wish. But when the exercise of silence is not yet perfect, then
some faculties speak often and despite us. Recollection becomes
difficult and almost always defective. It is never of long duration.
As this state is habitual, especially at the beginning of the way of
perfection, it is necessary to study recollection. It is question here
of knowing how to absorb the faculties according to one's desires
and how to keep others quiet.

Recollection is the application that is made of all the faculties after having imposed the silences. Thus we give ourselves to the object determined by the will, to God in prayer, to the sciences in study, etc.

We have said that recollection does not have God essentially for its object and that we can be recollected without thinking of God. Yet, considering recollection in relation to us, and as a religious virtue, it ought to have God for object in this sense that it helps us to place ourselves and then keep ourselves in the presence of God. Thus, if we apply ourselves to study, we do not give ourselves so completely that we do not keep at least an indirect thought of God as when we consider a picture in front of us, the person standing to the side is nevertheless seen from the corner of our eye.

D. OBEDIENCE

The third Virtue of Preparation is obedience by which we give ourselves into the hands of our superiors that they might help us conquer our nature and indicate the remedies which we do not have the courage to adopt ourselves. [For nonreligious this virtue could be best practiced by obedience to the confessor or spiritual director, for he has the same purpose as the confessor or spiritual director has among those whom he tries to guide to a higher spiritual level of perfection.]

The lack of a guide in our conduct has two principal inconveniences. First of all, left to ourselves, we are less inclined to take the route parallel and analogous to that taken by persons with whom we should be advancing. Second, we tend by ourselves to decide our conduct according to our impressions which incline us more readily toward vice.

E. SUPPORT OF MORTIFICATIONS

The virtue that we call support of mortifications is that virtue by which we suffer with patience in view of God whatever happens that is painful to our nature and offensive to our self-love. At this point in the plan of conduct, it is easy to understand that the support of mortifications is a favorable disposition to accomplish what the other exercises to this point have not been able to control.

There are five types of mortification under this heading: interior sufferings, exterior sufferings, trials, penitence, and reproaches.

II. Virtues of Purification

The Preparation virtues have brought the individual to sufficient self-knowledge that he is able to detect the obstacles that hinder him from progressing in virtue. But it is now necessary to go further to attack these vices and imperfections which form in us the Old Man.

Purification consists in an assiduous work that one performs on oneself by exact examens to discover the roots of evil and their characteristics. The Preparation has only cut the branches. In the Purification we search out the little roots to destroy them. The root of our vices is like the dogtooth grass, that destructive weed which grows so close to the earth that if one has the misfortune to leave even a very small leaf in the ground, it reproduces immediately and the field where it is left, a week afterward, is covered with this weed in greater quantity than before. It is the same for our vices. If we only cut them off, or when we root them out, if we leave some hidden in the earth of our hearts, we will accomplish nothing. For that purpose we must examine in the Purification not only the evidences, but also the causes which bring about these exterior effects.

The Virtues of Preparation make us know what we are, help us to discover our faults. But the Virtues of Purification go to the depths and eradicate the last filaments of the vices that are within us.

Then for the first time the silence of passions is controlled, the interior voice of God is heard and His exterior counsels obeyed, the irascible parts of the soul are calmed. We can now search out our faults, discover their causes.

    A. THE VIRTUES THAT PURIFY THE SOUL
      1. Interior obstacles of weakness
        Remedies: faith and fortitude

Since the sin of Adam our weakness is such that we can do
nothing for salvation without the particular assistance of God. Despite our continually formed good desires and resolutions we see
ourselves falling daily. It is said that the just man sins seven
times a day. This proves the great weakness of man. How many
serious falls do we not see, even among the greatest saints. Look
at St. Peter, the chief of the Church who had protested that he
would follow his master even to death. At the voice of a simple
servant he commits a frightful denial of his Savior, a denial that
cost him many tears. Consider our present state. What can we
do with such a great enemy?

There is not true virtue other than that which comes from
God and which rests firmly on Him alone. Virtues which recognize any other origin and which are founded on a different basis,
quickly manifest their weakness.

We can conquer our weaknesses by confidence in God, by a
habitual recourse to Him in prayer. Our falls always come because
we rely on ourselves. We believe that we can do something of
our own strength.

The remedy that we ought to bring to our weakness is a great
confidence in God who is all-powerful and who desires to assist
us. Of ourselves we can do nothing but fall; trusting in God, who
can harm us? Each time that God commands something He places
His grace on the side of his command. Do you think that God
does not know that you are incapable of executing what He desires of you? He has the intention of helping you provided that
you ask His help with a trusting confidence. Have then this
confidence.

Confidence in God in the work of Purification is a disposition,
a motive of the spiritual life, derived from and founded on the
virtues of faith and hope, and specifically aimed at overcoming our
weakness in acquiring and persevering in virtue. As the Apostle
says, if we can do nothing in ourselves we can do all in Him who
strengthens us. And as much as we are weak when left to ourselves so much do we become powerful when we lean upon the
arm of God.

With an unshakable confidence, expect everything from God,

our good and tender Father. Expect nothing good from yourself. The better you know yourself, the less confidence you will have in your own strength.

2. Evil inclinations
Remedy: worthy tendencies

The second enemy that wars against us is our evil inclinations. Truly, we have only to enter within ourselves and examine our heart. What do we see? Only evil inclinations, perverse penchants toward all that is evil. I have known a priest, and I have even confessed to him, who edified me the first time I saw him. He fulfilled his duties well but nevertheless he had something in his actions, difficult to describe or identify, that gave a presentiment of danger. I repulsed these thoughts, however, and chased them from my mind. But I was not wrong. Unhappily, this priest became one of the most outspoken enemies of religion in the French Revolution that persecuted the clergy. He found himself guided by his evil penchants when the Revolution arrived and little by little he was led along by them until finally the torrent engulfed him. He was completely lost and became as wicked as he previously had been good. It is this fact that is often seen. The more precious the liquor, the more completely it corrupts.

Think of a person who has the penchant of disguising things in regards to his director, of using devious methods which come from the inclinations of self-love. This individual should combat them by showing a great candidness of soul toward the director, making known to him his least dispositions. This should be done to a greater extent than if one were not troubled by this disease.

It is necessary then: (a) to know our evil inclinations; (b) to scorn them; (c) to act against them by posing as often as possible acts that are particularly contrary to them.

3. Incertitudes of conduct
Remedy: spiritual direction

With the first two points covered — living in a firm confidence in God and fostering our more worthy tendencies — it would seem that there would be no incertitude in our conduct. However, it must be admitted that feeble human reason easily hesitates when it does not have the way clearly outlined for the continued advancement in perfection.

What is the source of these incertitudes that prevent us from advancing? It is pride which does not wish to seek humbly the guidance of another, or having this guidance believes it knows better. If I wish to find alone a house that is located in a district unknown to me, it will take a good deal of time. Instead of following on a straight course, I take a way that turns and when I think that I have arrived, I find perhaps that I am a long way from my destination. I have walked and fatigued myself for nothing.

Incertitude of conduct is remedied by the opening of one's soul. Thus there is necessity of direction and of complete docility in order to avoid all false steps of scrupulosity, illusions.

To act for God, to humiliate oneself, to reveal one's interior to another. These are the three means of purifying the soul of weak virtue, evil penchants, and incertitudes. Thus, the intention of acting only and always for God and the confidence in the grace of God renders our virtues strong and solid. The intimate persuasion that we are nothing and that we can do nothing without God preserves us from all excess, from all light-mindedness, from all precipitation and trouble. The submission to the decisions of our director and a sincere revelation of all that occasions our incertitudes in conduct, gives us peace of soul and takes away from us all fear, all doubt. This is the way we perfect and purify the interior.

B. Virtues Which Precaution the Soul Against Exterior Obstacles
1. Contrarieties
Remedy: enduring patience

There are many kinds of contrarieties in this world. Some are very long and truly painful. Each has his own in life, or he will have them. There are some contrarieties on very important matters but these arrive more rarely. Daily, however, there are contrarieties on little things that can be found almost at each instant.

I once knew a priest who said to me one day that he was able to see the reason for his sickness. "I thank the Lord each day that He has sent me this malady," remarked the priest. "It has helped me to realize that everything is but nothing. Only the eternal is truly great and powerful and worthy of appreciation. I find myself of an entirely different frame of mind since God has tried me with this sickness." Therefore, trials purify the just and render them more saintly.

This long patience, the remedy to our contrarieties, enables us to acquire a treasure of merits and enriches us for heaven. The different contrarieties of which our life is full are for us a means of recompense.

2. Suggestions of the worldly-minded
Remedy: Maxims of the Bible, search for truth, renewal of resolutions

When nature finds itself wearied and is tempted to revolt, suggestions soon arise within oneself or come from the outside.

A person says to us: "You are scrupulous to be so exact in silence. The Rule forbids speaking but we can say a few words here and there without failing against it." Another time in recreation under pretext that the Rule prescribes gaiety and even laughing, someone suggests that we are not wrong to laugh with boisterous show as long as it gives us a certain relaxation. We can abstain from this exercise of self-control and dispense ourselves from the Rule for this time. Finally, how many thousand and one little things that appear as nothing but which lead to relaxation can impress us and convince a heart that is weak and lacking in generosity.

As a remedy it is necessary to recall the solid principles and hold firm against these dangerous suggestions and other maxims which have an appearance of truth but which are in reality false. We must recall that in such and such a retreat or such and such a meditation, I have seen this matter in this way and took such a resolution. Why now do I see differently?

3. Temptations
Remedies: Spiritual combat and flight

The third exterior enemy of the combat is that of temptations. They ought to be combated very often by mere scorn. Since the temptations come from the demon who is the father of lies and of pride, nothing confuses and sends him into flight so easily as the scorn that one manifests for him and the evil things he has inspired. When tempted, we should also have recourse to God who is all our strength.

III. Virtues of Consummation

From all the documents that could be found on advancement to the Virtues of Consummation, it would seem that the individual must make certain that the first two sets of virtues have been quite well acquired. The signs of readiness to proceed into the Virtues of Consummation are: a reliance upon the grace of God, call upon the intercession of Christ and Mary, and finally the suggestion of the director to advance into this rare state of perfection. There must also be ardent frequent reception of the sacraments, greater exactitude in spiritual exercises and prayers, more habitual conversation with God during the day, calm in all the movements of the soul, and quickness to obey. Thus, in general, the individual shows at all times that the "Old Man is strongly under control."

A. HUMILITY

By definition this virtue is the recognition of our nothingness in all things.

For the abasement which procures in all things Christian humility, we must always have present to ourselves the cause from which all comes, that sustains all things — God. As a consequence we must attribute nothing to ourselves. All comes from God.

If you are convinced of the nothingness of man and that grace penetrates in solitude, close your ears to the subtle accents of idolatry. Consider as idolatry every praise which is not addressed to God and God alone. Pray for those who err. Abjure the opinion that one wishes to share with you. From the depths of your heart and mouth, if you have a right to speak, say with conviction "God is all and we are nothing." Among those who are admitted to work at their Consummation in virtue, it is necessary to make a study to correct and change all language which tends, however little, to adulation.

B. INTERIOR MODESTY

Here the habitual sentiment of modesty is meant, that which becomes a profound virtue of the soul. Modesty is the manner of accepting and sustaining the advantages that we must believe are not due to us. It is the virtue par excellence of the Blessed Virgin who has reunited the greatest favors and the most outstanding qualities to the most profound self-abasement and to an entire abjection in the view of the divine majesty.

This virtue is a state in which we leave unknown or in which we hide the advantages of mind and body, such as beauty, talents, virtue, birth, fortune, rank, dignities, etc. The habit of favoring and establishing this state is that which constitutes the virtue of modesty. The modest person regards all these pretended advantages as so many shadows, not finding anything except vanity of vanities, according to the expression of the Book of Wisdom.

C. SELF-ABNEGATION

It has three major features:

1. of the mind and personal judgment;
2. of natural inclinations, tastes, and attractions which are not according to God and His graces;
3. of spiritual consolations.

The virtue of self-abnegation effects the complete detachment from all personal qualities.

D. RENOUNCEMENT OF CREATURES AND THE WORLD

By this virtue we renounce all the vanities and bonds that hold us to the earth and to the things of the earth.

IV. Conclusion

A. In Conformity With Jesus Christ and Mary

Jesus Christ kept silence and recollection during the greater part of His life. He spoke with men only in order to instruct them fully in a few words. His soul was carried toward exterior things only in order to operate miracles. He was recollected toward His Father, to whom He wished to be obedient until the death of the cross. He was not less obedient as man to St. Joseph His guardian and to the Blessed Virgin His Mother in the natural order for the most common works of life. Mortifications were His ordinary portion. True Lamb of God, He drank the chalice of bitterness, submitting Himself to ignominies and to death while crying "My Father, if it is your will, may your will be done."

The entire life of the Blessed Virgin on earth is the lesson of silence, of the most profound recollection, of a perfect submission. It presents a long chain of unparalleled mortifications supported without murmuring that carries to the very death of her Son on the cross.

B. A Lifetime Venture

It is not to be expected that in the rather short term of say a retreat or a novitiate the subjects are able to be carried to a high point of perfection in all the virtues and all of the holy practices which have just been rapidly indicated. It suffices that each of them possess clearly in mind the method and understands the extent of the enterprise. It has been remarked that on some of these virtues it is the affair of a lifetime to acquire them in full measure of grace and according to the capacity of our hearts.

CHAPTER TWO

Mental Prayer

To advance beyond the spiritual life of most Christians which consists mainly in obeying the Commandments, the individual must use mental prayer. In fact, it is a necessary requisite for any real advancement in spiritual life, both for the religious and the Christian in the world, because without it the soul does not live in close continual union with God. Mental prayer is made stronger by continual use, just as strength is increased in the human body by nourishment and exercise. Once Father Chaminade had introduced his spiritual subjects to the System of Virtues, he immediately prepared them by stages to make more and more mental prayer.

The immediate and final result of mental prayer was the Life of Faith which is at once associated with the presence of God. Thus, perfection for him consisted in walking continually by a life of faith in the presence of God. This walking in the presence of God, he frequently pointed out will be also our reward in heaven, perfected, however, in every possible manner.

In the following two chapters, we shall listen to Father Chaminade explain how we should go about making mental prayer according to his tried method. In the chapter following this one, we shall continue to consider mental prayer, but in connection with the spirit of faith and the presence of God.

I. NATURE OF PRAYER

Two essential and fundamental truths are that we are not able to save ourselves except through grace and we are not able to obtain grace except through prayer. "Without me you can do nothing" (Jn. 15:5). We ought always to pray (cf. Lk. 18:1). Since grace is a necessity, prayer is necessarily a duty. Nothing can replace prayer, because it takes the place of everything else, and because it is a duty necessary for the fulfillment of all the others.

Prayer is at the same time the practice and the stay of all the virtues; in fact, prayer exercises and nourishes virtue. The Christian is then by spiritual vocation, by duty, by self-interest, and by gratitude a man of prayer.

Interior prayer which places the soul in communication with God, if it is not zeal itself, is the proximate cause of zeal. Thus prayer and zeal can be said to be inseparable. In fact, it is from this that a prayer well made can be distinguished from all that is an imitation of it. True prayer is followed immediately by zeal while the other rests without effect. Thus true prayer is the source of zeal and will sometimes be taken for it.

To make mental prayer is to raise our mind and heart to God, to penetrate ourselves in His presence with reflections, aided by His light, on various truths meant to make us better.

"Raise our mind and heart to God." It is to detach our mind from the things of earth as though forgotten that we might occupy ourselves in the presence of God by letting our heart be touched by the sentiments of respect and love which that presence ought to inspire.

"To penetrate ourselves in His presence." Without losing sight of Him, acting with Him and having Him act with us; in other words, not to content ourselves with raising our mind to God but applying and attaching it to Him.

"With reflection aided by His light." Such are the consequences and unfolding of this elevation and application of our mind to God. Our soul exercises its faculties; it considers, it compares, it judges, it reasons. It does this before God and under the influence of the spirit of God; it invokes Him from the beginning, it consults Him without end, it beseeches Him at every instant to enlighten its darkness, resolve its doubts, dissipate its errors.

"On various truths meant to make us better." This indicates the object and the goal of mental prayer. One can also render God

His due; in fact, one ought to do so. But such is no more than a manner relative to the needs of our soul.

Persons but little versed in the ways of God speak of mental prayer as an exercise in which only a certain class of persons can succeed. They imagine that learning is an indispensable condition for mental prayer. They claim that an ignorant man, though sufficiently instructed as to his religious duties, is unfit for mental prayer. Strange delusion, perfidious ruse of the spirit of darkness! When, this ordinary man, this poor layman, who, let us suppose, cannot even read, is called to see God in heaven, to love Him, and to praise Him like you; he is called, as well as you, to know God, to love Him, and to serve Him here below, and you would declare him unfit for mental prayer, that is, for an exercise the only end of which is to learn to know God and one's own self? To be consistent, say rather, if you dare that he is unfit to know God, unfit to love Him, unfit to serve Him, or that he is doomed to serve God and to love Him without knowing Him. No doubt, he is unfit for that kind of mental prayer which is rather the work of the mind than of God, which is more like a theological or philosophical thesis than a consideration of faith; but this manner of mental prayer is nothing but a more or less dry study, into which the intellect and judgment enter for more than faith and the heart. I admit that he is happily unfit for such meditation, because it is rather a danger than a real advantage. I admit also that he is probably unfit for that sublime mental prayer which has been attained by Thomases, the Bonaventures, the Bernards. But what do I venture to say with such assurance? Can I doubt his ability to rise to a degree so sublime, since, after all, it is the Holy Spirit Himself which instructs the upright and simple soul in the pious exercise of mental prayer? The examples of so many holy anchorites, of most of the monks that people the deserts and were lacking the most rudimentary knowledge; the examples of the greatest saints, such as those of an Anthony, a Francis of Assisi, an Ignatius, a Rodriguez; finally the example of so many persons of ordinary education, and nevertheless so familiar with the most sublime paths of mental prayer; do not so many examples prove the contrary of what I was about to assert? Read the lives of the

Fathers of the desert and the lives of the saints, and then tell me whether you still hold persons of little education, like the ordinary faithful, still unfit for mental prayer! If the best mental prayer were that in which the soul develops the most beautiful and correct considerations, then we might be forced to conclude that the contemplation is not so perfect, because in it the soul is like an idiot — pardon the expression — that only beholds, without inquiring about the how and the wherefore. But such a conclusion runs counter to the principles that we have enunciated at the beginning of this discussion.

Mental prayer is a hallowed conversation of the soul with its God, an unutterable conversation in which a God does not disdain to make Himself known to a vile creature and to initiate it in the depths of His eternal designs. It is a conversation in which the soul, after having contemplated by the light of faith the infinite and adorable perfections of the Divinity, the plans of His Wisdom, and the economy of His works, humbles and annihilates itself at the sight of its weakness. Who can tell what passes in a soul enlightened by faith in the presence of its God? What inexpressible delight, what pure joy, what tenderness in the very tears it sheds! And then, what knowledge is granted it in proportion as it loses itself in the contempt and oblivion of all that is not God. What knowledge is granted of God, in whom the soul continually discovers new features of loveliness; knowledge of itself, revealing more thoroughly its own nothingness and abjection; knowledge of creatures from whom it readily detaches itself. The heart is purified, faith is increased; and the soul, continuing faithful to grace, will soon arrive at the happy state in which, lost in God, it is completely oblivious of itself, contemplating and making others contemplate His infinite perfections.

Exercise for the soul in making mental prayer does not remain inactive in an absolute repose; it acts, it exercises its powers of the soul and not of the body, which should pretty well be counted as nothing. The posture assumed, however, can facilitate or hamper the attention of the soul by reason of some distraction or physical inconvenience. Which raises itself toward God? The soul leaves aside all earthly and perishable things to raise itself toward the object of its eternal happiness, toward its Sovereign Good; it abandons to the earth its body, its humiliating prison, and transports itself to heaven for a foretaste of its destiny and anticipation of paradise. And, in fact, does it not taste this happiness as much as it is possible here below? It is with its God, it sees Him, it speaks to Him.

It is He who, by a sweet impulsion of His grace, invites the soul and says to it, as the Spouse says to His bride: "Come my beloved friend!" All that the soul has of facility in raising itself to God, all that it feels of consolation in its union with Him has been sent and given to it by God. If it rise to God, it is due to His coming down to draw it up. If it be united to Him, it is due to His embrace of love.

We would fall into a dangerous illusion if we remained in an absolute repose while waiting for God to do everything. He would do nothing, and the devil would do a great deal. It is not that God could not raise us up to Himself without any effort on our part, but ordinarily He does not wish to; if sometimes He does so, we ought not to await such action and count on it.

An eagle has no trouble flying when it is high in the air. But, even though it be capable of rising very high, what pain it must give itself to get off the ground! It makes a long take-off to get its wings in motion; for, not finding enough air to launch itself right away into the sky, it must exert itself to get there. There you have what the soul must do in mental prayer; and there you will find the work of man.

God is incontestably the principle and the necessary principle of mental prayer, that is, there can be no true prayer without God as principle. But He is not the only principle. Mental prayer is simultaneously the work of God and of man. God, who created us without our co-operation, will not save us without our co-operation. He will raise us to Himself and unite us to Him only insofar as we present ourselves to Him and direct our powers of soul to Him.

We should not seek other knowledge through our considerations in mental prayer than that which faith gives us. We should not excite our will except by the motives suggested by faith. We ought not to reject the light which the Holy Spirit would communicate to our understanding through the gifts of understanding, wisdom, knowledge, and counsel or the warning impressions which He would give to our will through the gifts of fortitude, piety, and the fear of the Lord. But of ourselves, we should hold to faith.

It would be a strange delusion to apply ourselves to mental prayer for the sake of consolation, to gain the confidence and esteem of men, to appear wise in our own eyes, or for any other motive not referring exclusively to our salvation and the glory of God. We do not take up the practice of mental prayer in order to become more learned, but to become more humble, more holy, more solid in our resolutions, disabused of the false enlightenment of our deluded intellect and of a corrupt world.

We must make mental prayer with the intention of becoming better, on the one hand better to know our duties, the virtues for which we must strive, the models we should imitate; on the other hand, better to be convinced of our weakness, our misery, our needs, our defects, our imperfections, and our vices. We go to mental prayer as to a fountain that will allay our thirst forevermore; as to a fire, to rekindle our fervor; as to a remedy, to heal our infirmities; as to a repast, to eat the daily bread which the heavenly Father distributes. This right and pure intention is of the highest importance; it must not be lost sight of.

The great advantage which we derive from mental prayer does not proceed from our facility to think, to consider, to feel, in one word, to occupy ourselves; but from being before God and with God. We must believe that God works in us, though insensibly.

Thus it is that, in mental prayer, the soul attains to the knowledge of God and of itself; and these two attainments are so closely intertwined that, to advance in one, is to advance also in the other. By contemplating the infinite perfections of the Divine, the soul grows stronger in His love and becomes capable of greater sacrifices. As the soul knows itself better, it will abase and annihilate itself more and more as the conviction and clear evidence of its weakness, its miseries and its imperfections grow upon it. From this, there is but one step to desiring and earnestly demanding of Heaven contempt and hatred of self. The knowledge of God and of its own nothingness convince it more and more of the hideousness and the hatefulness of attacking an infinite Majesty, of offending Sanctity par excellence, and of defying the most terrible justice; of the crime of a vile creature which has nothing, can do nothing, which depends altogether on Him whom it outrages and receives everything from Him, even the very faculty which it abuses to offend Him. Then its sorrow grows, its regrets become keener, its heart is torn; it cries to Heaven to implore grace and constitutes itself the minister of the Lord's vengeance. Then its humility takes root; penance and mortification are endeared to it; it blesses Providence in the troubles provided for it. Then the heart is purified, divine love is enthroned, and the soul begins to have a foretaste of heaven.

Although we can say that all in man must pray to make a good meditation, only the soul rises up to God and, for that purpose, uses all its faculties — memory, imagination, understanding, will, and sensitive appetite — with a marvelous subordination and harmony.

The memory works first and furnishes to the understanding the material of the considerations. The understanding acts in connection with the imagination and uses its images either to know various objects, to form a sound judgment on them, to draw forth solid conclusions, or to attach itself to them in a simple contemplation which is as the heart or its repose. The will follows upon the understanding and produces hope, or other similar movements born of the diversity of objects proposed by the understanding, sometimes stronger, sometimes weak and slow depending on the application and disposition of the mind. Finally, the sensitive appetite joins itself to the will in a secret alliance, which, however, is not so close that the higher part of the soul can excite the lower whenever it wishes; it is not so close either that the higher part is the captain of the imagination, which wanders off frequently and thereby troubles the harmonious concert in mental prayer.

If the divine light is necessary to our understanding in the practice of mental prayer, the fire of the Holy Spirit is still more necessary to excite the will, because it is more difficult to love humility, patience, mortification, evangelical poverty, and all the virtues regarding which the will is to make strong resolutions during meditation, than merely to ponder over them or to perceive the beauties of them. "We have the faculty of our free will," says St. Bernard, "but we have not the power to accomplish what we will. The will exists by the Creator's favor; it acts rightly by the Savior's grace, and it fails by its own cowardice. We are free in the movements of our will; but it is by grace that we will what is good."

In heaven we shall see God intuitively; we shall see Him face to face in His nature and in His essence. From such an entirely blessed vision will result an immense love as extensive and as strong as our power to love. Made to love, but to love only what is truly lovable, our heart will seize with irresistible force the object whose infinite lovableness the mind displays. In the transports of its intoxication, the heart will praise and exalt the unspeakable perfection of its Beloved. Lost in God as in an ocean of light, wholly overwhelmed by the ravishing splendor of the Divinity, our intelligence will be eternally absorbed in an ecstatic contemplation which will furnish an everlasting aliment for the divine flame which will devour our heart without consuming it.

The end of mental prayer is to raise the soul to the Infinite Being, to render homage to Him, to converse with Him, to unite oneself to Him with all one's strength, to advance His glory through an increase of knowledge and love of Him, to transform oneself into Him and become an image of His divine perfections through the practice of the most excellent virtues, and to treat with Him not only of one's own salvation and perfection but also the salvation of all mankind.

"My heart grew hot within me, and in my meditation a fire shall flame out." Do you believe that this text is applicable only to the holy Prophet who uttered it? It may be applied to every person who, following his example, seeks to inflame his heart during his ordinary actions and endeavors to enkindle it with love by means of a good meditation. It is in prayer that God is pleased to communicate Himself to him and that he finds the strength and aid necessary to surmount the obstacles to his salvation.

If every Christian who is desirous of corresponding to the designs of God on himself ought to make use of the great means of mental prayer, what should not a religious do? What would

his state be without mental prayer? Can anyone comprehend how
there could be solid virtue without fidelity to this holy exercise?
No, it is not possible for anyone to persevere for any length of
time in virtue if he neglect to make mental prayer.

All the good that we affect in others depends on the assiduity
and care that we bring to meditation; for, even if we would do
some good by means of the grace of our state, which is attached
to the character with which we are invested, it would be very
little in comparison with what God would have done through us
if we had been faithful.

Let us then make real mental prayer; I say real mental prayer,
because we would make a sad affair of it if we would pass the
time of mental prayer in such a way as to accomplish nothing, for
the fruit drawn from it does not depend on the time that we
devote to it, but on the manner in which we employ the time.
If we do not know how to make mental prayer we must seek for
instruction, we must ask and consult, and, when once instructed
on this important matter, we must carry out the instruction and
persevere, despite the obstacles that the devil might raise up in
our path. For the devil is thoroughly aware that if we perform our
mental prayer well, we shall produce much fruit in souls, and that,
if he could prevent us from practicing it, or disgust us with it
by reason of the obstacles that he opposes to it, our efforts to
snatch his prey from him would be unavailing.

II. METHOD OF MEDITATION

There are many methods of mental prayer and yet few men of
prayer. What is the reason? Is it the fault of the methods or
that of the persons who follow them? Perhaps it is the fault of
both together? It is not for us to pronounce on the matter. The
men of God who have left methods have had uncommon lights
on the ways of perfection. To blame the means they have left us
for making progress would be a sign of pride and a lack of respect
due to them. Let us recognize and not fear to avow that these
methods in general are good, very good even, and capable of con-
ducting us to the highest forms of prayer.

Although we may fully praise these methods, let us not attach undue importance to them. Let us not believe that the pious authors were so mistaken as not to suspect that there could be any better methods. The many variable methods do not suit all times, all places, or all persons. The end and aim of the methods are to teach the individual to converse with God, to give the soul as it were, the rudiments of mental prayer, to direct it and to guide its first steps in the holy exercise. When, however, the soul has had some practice in meditation, the methods cease to have the same importance. Eventually they may even be abandoned as the child gives up the hand of the mother once it has learned to walk by itself. Our method is to have no method; or, if the name of method is to be given to the practice we are about to make known, then here is our method of mental prayer.

Three principal things go to make up the exercise of meditation: the considerations, the affections, and the resolutions, and they must be so united that the considerations are made only for the affections, and the affections only for the resolutions.

The following outline is Father Chaminade's most original work on mental prayer. It is the method he thought best for his followers who were lay and religious men of action in the salvation of the world.

Title: Mental Prayer of the Common Method

I. Nature of Prayer

To elevate the heart and spirit to God; to detach ourselves from the earth in order to penetrate ourselves with His presence through our reflections aided by His light — the exercises of our faculties; the work of God and man — fundamental principle of prayer.

II. Dispositions for Prayer, Remote Preparation

God is always ready, not man; man must prepare his heart and his spirit:

a) Disposition of the heart — purity

b) Disposition of the spirit — faith, recollection. Faith is acquired by prayer and repeated acts; recollection is acquired by silence.

III. Choice of the Subject, Proximate Preparation

Generally it is not God but we who must prepare the subject:

a) Three kinds of subjects — (1) a word of Scripture; (2) the consideration of some truth, independent of a text; (3) the reproduction of a mystery of our Lord or the Blessed Virgin; before prayer it is necessary to choose the subject in relation with the fruits to be attained.

b) Subjects by rank in the Way to Perfection: (1) for beginners — truths of faith, grandeurs of Jesus and Mary, last ends, paradise; (2) purgative way — sin, Passion of Christ, mercy of God; (3) illuminative way — life of our Lord, the Blessed Virgin; the choice of the subject supposes the knowledge of the state one is in.

IV. Order of the Prayer

a) Immediate preparation, interior — two acts:

1. Put oneself in the presence of God — we must render our duties to our God, our Father, and our Judge; join to the presence of God the presence of Mary.

2. Ask His assistance — through the merits of Christ and the intercession of Mary while invoking the Holy Spirit.

b) Body of the prayer

1. Considerations

If on the word of Scripture — discover the meaning, make acts of faith. If on some truth — examine the importance, the circumstances, the reasons. If on a mystery of our Lord — represent the mystery, who, what, where. The general means that one should use in making the considerations might also be the following: examine the general sense; examine the special meaning of some words; contemplate and reconstruct the facts; and, if a beginner, apply all the senses.

2. Affections

They differ according to the subjects; beginners should again use the senses.

3. Resolutions

Because the end of prayer is to make us better; reflect to see what is lacking in one's life in regard to the subject meditated on; resolutions must be particular, present, efficacious.

c) Conclusion

This part is more important than we might first think.

1. Thank God
2. Confess our faults and humble ourselves
3. Choose a spiritual bouquet
4. Put all in the hands of Mary

V. Examination of the Mental Prayer

a) On the habitual dispositions or remote preparation
b) On the preparation of the subject
c) On the order of the prayer
d) On the cause of the distractions
e) On the resolutions or spiritual bouquet

As for the considerations, Father Chaminade well realized that the novice or the beginner would have very little upon which to draw his meditation. Wisely he instructed the novices to make mixed mental prayer until such time that they felt sure enough to abandon this means of meditating. In this he agreed with St. Teresa of Avila who said she used mixed mental prayer for most of the first fifteen years of her religious life.

By mixed mental prayer I understand a prayer that is partly vocal, partly mental. He who would enter into the ways of prayer ought to begin with mixed prayer on the Apostles' Creed.

By this meditative reading I mean a prayer which is at once

vocal and mental. Let us take, as an example, the first of the
Penitential Psalms: "O Lord, rebuke me not in thy indignation,
nor chastise me in thy wrath. Have mercy on me, O Lord, for I
am weak; heal me, O Lord, for my bones are troubled. And my
soul is troubled exceedingly; but thou, O Lord, how long?" — With
a sentiment of repentance pronounce the words of the first verse:
"O Lord, rebuke me not in thy indignation, etc." Then dwell on
them for some moments, repeat them mentally; then pass on to
the second verse, thus passing from one verse to the next and to
the end of the psalm.

The first principal part in the Considerations consists in re-
viewing our Savior Jesus Christ in relation to the subject of our
meditation and to properly acknowledge Him. In the second part
we must do three things: (a) convince ourselves that what we
have considered in the first point is of great importance; (b) that
we have need of it; (c) and to ask God for it with fervor. The
third point consists in taking a firm resolution.

It is of elementary importance to remember at the beginning
of mental prayer that God, who sees and hears us, is there and,
to give thought to this, we at once pay Him our homage. These
duties which we owe to God when we present ourselves before
Him for mental prayer flow from His three relations to us. He is
our God, our Father, and our Judge. Before God we humbly pros-
trate ourselves in the sentiment and posture of adoration; to our
Father, we offer our hearts in confidence; before our Judge, we
confess our past iniquities and our actual miseries.

It is good that we examine in what manner we ought to make
our meditations in order to preserve ourselves from the illusion
of the evil spirit who only too often finds means to introduce
himself into our holiest actions in order to prevent, or at least
to diminish, their happy effects.

Now, observe an infallible principle which will shelter us from
his cunning and from all illusion; it consists in having our meditation based on some truth of faith, as, for instance, on these
words so consoling, which our Lord Jesus Christ will say on the
last day to His elect: "Come, ye blessed of my Father, possess
the kingdom prepared for you from the foundations of the world."

We shall, then, have this as our very simple method of making meditation. It shall be befitting all classes of persons, even the most ignorant, and, nevertheless, the noblest, safe from all illusion, leading straight to God and assuring great progress in virtue. This will consist in meditating in the light of faith, in often renewing our acts of faith in the truth on which we are meditating, and in drawing therefrom a practical resolution which we will put in execution at least from one meditation to the next, thus making practice follow upon the meditation and meditation upon practice; an excellent method in order not to abuse the favor that God grants us in admitting us to an audience with Himself.

Let us suppose you wish to meditate on heaven. Represent to yourself Jesus Christ asking you whether you believe that there is a heaven, that during all eternity the saints will there be overwhelmed in a torrent of delights. Reply to the Lord: "Yes, I believe it!" Furthermore, do you believe that you have been created to enjoy this happiness? Make acts of faith also on this point, and think on the means that you ought to employ to attain this end.

We have several examples in the Gospel which prove how agreeable this practice is to God, and, among others, that of Martha. When, after the death of her brother, she learned that our divine Savior had come to Bethany, she ran to meet Him, and, having cast herself at His feet, said to Him: "Lord, if thou hadst been here, my brother would not have died!" Jesus answered her: "Thy brother shall rise again." "Yes, Lord," she answered, "and we all shall rise on the last day." "I am," Jesus said, "the resurrection and the life; believest thou this?" "Yes, Lord, I believe it," answered Martha.

The highest degree of mental prayer is that of pure love, the unique feature of which is to unite us intimately with God and to transform us into Himself. This is brought about in meditation by the gift of wisdom which leads us to contemplate Jesus Christ as the glory of the Father, divesting us, so to say, of our gross and terrestrial being and endowing us with one celestial and divine, so that it is no longer the old man that lives in us, but the new, and also the new man will keep on growing ever more and more

by a process of spiritual enlightenment, in proportion to our progress in union with God by contemplation, until finally we arrive
at perfect holiness.

Having attained this height, should the soul still make use of
the method we have outlined? We do not intend to reject the
method of meditation that we have set down; but we must not
confound meditation itself with the method of meditation. In this
case it were well to use, but with prudence and discretion, the
means which the method furnishes us for considering better the
truths which faith proposes to us, for guiding the affections of
our hearts and for strengthening our resolutions. The preparatory
acts will also prove useful.

But when man feels himself drawn along by God, he must not
think of carrying out his own way; for him, it is important, in this
case, to be docile to the will of God and not to desire in meditation aught else but what the good Lord wishes; the so-called
meditation of discourse is useless and even harmful when the Spirit
of God works within us.

III. ANALYSIS OF THE METHOD OF MENTAL PRAYER

*Let us now take the method of Father Chaminade as given several
pages above and let him analyze the various parts.*

A. Remote Preparation

To enter mental prayer without preparation and without pre-
disposition is, according to Scripture, to tempt God. God makes
such great promises for prayer only inasmuch as the soul praying
has certain dispositions or neglects nothing to clothe itself in them.
"Before prayer prepare thy soul, and be not as a man that tempts
God" (Ecclus. 18:23).

"Though I did almost nothing in my meditation," says the soul
who consoles himself for his little success in mental prayer, "and
was almost continually lost in distractions or preoccupations, I was
calm. I even believe I had done a good work and made a sacrifice
— that of my annoyance and weariness — in going punctually to
mental prayer. I was well aware that a preparation was necessary,

but I was contented with that which forms a part of the meditation itself. I scarcely ever went further than that, and often I made even this preparation almost without being conscious of it. I consoled myself, for I would gladly have prayed and been without distraction; besides I have often been told to look upon these distractions as trials sent by God."

To all this I can only answer, to enter upon prayer in such a way, without preparation and without the right disposition, is truly, in the words of Scripture, to tempt God.

God is ever ready to receive us, to listen to us, and to communicate His lights and gifts to us. If we ordinarily play such a feeble part, it is because we ourselves are not sufficiently prepared.

What are then the dispositions that God requires of man? We have seen that it is principally the mind and the heart that act in mental prayer. Man raises and attaches his mind to God because He believes in Him and knows Him; he raises his heart to God because he loves God and seeks Him.

The mind and the heart or, in the words of St. Teresa, the understanding and the will are the two wings by means of which the soul flies to God in order to repose in His bosom. They are the two instruments that man puts at the service of God so that God may act upon him; but it is necessary that man should previously apply himself to put these instruments in a suitable condition, which, however, he can only do with the grace of God.

As to the dispositions of the heart, it must be calm and detached from sin. How can a man agitated by some passion or affection for some sin attach his heart to God?

Purity, preserved from the time of baptism or recovered by penance, and the mortification of the passions will put the soul into this happy state of peace with God and love for Him. Mental prayer will be easier and more profitable in proportion as the heart is purer and the passions are more mortified.

We set it down as a principle that anyone who has not the happy habit of the presence of God will never really make mental prayer. He would be deceiving himself greatly in believing that it is enough to make a few acts of faith, of adoration, humility, and contrition before entering into the matter of his prayer. These acts formulated by a purely mechanical habit, would mean nothing, would recollect the soul only slightly or not at all, and would leave it open to dissipation. All the methods which urge certain preparatory acts presupposes the habit of the presence of God, without which the prescribed acts are altogether insignificant.

I remark that those who really want to make progress in mental prayer frequently exercise themselves over and above the time set apart for mental prayer in thoughts of God, so that, by the habit that grows upon them, they need less time to replace themselves in the presence of God, and in that way they can devote more time to the meditation proper.

Is not the need of this remote preparation a pious stratagem of the masters of the spiritual life to lead souls to the practice of virtue? Is there such a dependence between the labor of this preparation and mental prayer that the quality of the latter depends entirely on the former? Should he who has neglected it abstain from mental prayer?

No, the masters of the spiritual life prescribe this preparation only because of the intimate connection they perceive between it and mental prayer. Can man overdo the reverence he owes God and the interest he takes in the conversation he is to hold with His adorable Majesty? Everyone should say to himself with David: "It is not to receive the visit of some great man of this world that I am preparing myself, but to appear before the Sovereign Lord, the God infinitely holy."

Let us go into some particulars on preparation. The masters of spiritual life tell us that the principal disposition of mental prayer is purity of heart and the fervent practice of virtue. Are they not right? We draw near to the Lord in mental prayer in order to enjoy His divine colloquies. But only pure souls are permitted to approach Him. They must wash their garments and cleanse themselves from all impurities before they present themselves to Him. Mental prayer is the paradise on earth, but as nothing defiled may enter this paradise, we must be pure to gain access. We see and possess God, as it were, during mental prayer, but He will never suffer Himself to be seen and possessed, except by pure souls. They are like the chaste souls that keep themselves wholly for the Beloved, and their Beloved is also wholly theirs in mental prayer.

The masters of spiritual life tell us that, in order to draw near to the Lord during mental prayer, we must withdraw from creatures during the day, avoid frivolity, remain recollected. Is their statement not true? The Lord is a jealous God, who cannot suffer our souls, that have the honor of being His spouses, to seek their consolation elsewhere than with Him. If we seek Him after long and vain converse with creatures, He closes the door upon us and conceals Himself from us during our mental prayer. Moreover, the ideas which engrossed our mind during conversations annoy it during prayer and will not permit it to occupy itself with God; they are as a dense fog which conceals from our view this divine Sun. They are as clouds of troublesome flies that break up our repose, and will not allow us to apply ourselves to the consideration of the divine truths with the tranquillity necessary to relish them. Our imagination is like a mettlesome horse; if we permit it to break loose and roam about during the day, we are no longer its master and we will not be able to control it during mental prayer. It must be held in check during the remainder of the time, if it is not to escape during prayer.

From these details, you can readily perceive the intimate relation existing between mental prayer and the remote preparation. Even if you have neglected your preparation in part or in whole, you ought not to pass up your period of mental prayer. Instead you should: (a) humbly ask pardon of all the faults you have committed culpably since your last meditation and renew the resolution to be more faithful in the future; (b) bear all the difficulties you will meet in your meditation with patience and in the spirit of humility and penance; (c) and do all you can to employ your time well.

Recollection is the application of our faculties, after silence has been imposed upon them, to the object determined upon by the will. Considered as a religious virtue, recollection has God for its object, inasmuch as it aids us to place ourselves in the presence of God and to maintain ourselves therein, no matter what our occupation may be. For example, we recollect our mind for study; that is, we apply it to some reading; but we do not apply it so

exclusively thereto that we do not preserve indirectly a thought
of God, much as when we regard a picture that is before us, we
still see in a way the objects aside of it. Moreover, whatever may
engross our minds and our senses, by recollection, our hearts always
belong to God; for, as to our hearts, we may not admit anything
there, but God alone.

The means by which we may recollect ourselves vary according
to circumstances, and the circumstances we may reduce to five.
They are when we want to pray; when we go to recreation; when
we perform manual labor; when we apply ourselves to mental work;
finally when, in whatever circumstance it may be, our soul is agitated and distracted by some passion or preoccupation of the mind.

In mental prayer especially it is important to be recollected; it
is then that recollection should be more complete and is also much
easier; all the faculties of our soul should then be occupied with
God alone.

For this purpose, we must, after we have placed ourselves in
His presence and impressed it on our minds by a lively faith, draw
successively upon all our faculties. We must draw upon the memory,
to make it forget all else, and not to trouble, by irrelevant representations the conversation we are about to have with God; on
the imagination, to occupy it with God, with the magnificence of
the heavenly court, with the spectacle of the cross or some other
image that will captivate it and rivet it on God. We must also
draw upon the heart, elevating and uniting it to God by an act of
love; finally we must, in a measure, separate from ourselves, leave
our body, in order to place our souls in God, and there, by the
sentiment we have of His presence, commune with Him on the
subject of our meditation as has been pointed out in the method.

Distractions may come and overturn in a moment this whole
edifice of recollection. Without troubling ourselves, we must rebuild
it again and again, and not be wearied by the frequent repetition
of the struggle to build up a life of recollection. What has been
said here of mental prayer applies to all kinds of prayer.

During manual labor which demands no concentration of the
mind, recollection consists in: (a) giving sufficient attention to
our work; (b) raising our hearts to God by frequent acts of love;

(c) occupying our minds with some good thought, as the presence of God, the subject of the morning meditation, the malice of our sins, the blessings of our vocation, the graces we have to ask for ourselves or for others.

To do all this we must be masters of ourselves; we must from the beginning of the action have disposed our faculties in the way we will have them to act while the action lasts, and, from time to time, as we perceive these conditions to be disturbed, to restore them.

During study, recollection may be maintained much in the same way as during manual labor. Before study, we should raise our hearts to God; then apply our minds to the object of our study, keeping always in view the presence of God, and in our hearts the fire of His love, which is more necessary than during manual labor. Study should be interrupted occasionally to replace one's soul in this condition.

Notwithstanding these precautions, recollection is never so perfect during study, that those who devote themselves to it habitually do not risk to gradually lose their initial fervor. It is advisable, therefore, for them to stop from time to time a few moments to apply themselves wholly to mental prayer. As to what concerns recollection, teaching and preaching belong to the same class of occupations as study.

The recreations are moments very dangerous for recollection. They comprise walks, visits, all light conversations, all actions in which it is proper to unbend the faculties to recreate the mind.

The basis of recollection at such difficult times is the peace of the soul. If the soul is not at peace, if it be given up to dissipation, recollection will vanish. If, on the contrary, the soul is at peace, its tranquillity, joined to the absence of all contention, will be for it a sufficient recreation, and it will remain united with God, without other effort than a sweet, but habitual, elevation of its mind and heart to God, and a certain watchfulness over self.

There are circumstances under which the soul is so distracted, either by a passion which troubles the heart, or by an occupation which engrosses the mind, that, even in mental prayer, we can scarcely recollect ourselves for some moments.

In this irksome condition, we cannot succeed in controlling our faculties by complete recollection, such as is required in prayer. Indirectly the result can be achieved more easily. Manual labor, vocal prayer, a reading, will very well dispose us for mental prayer which will, in turn, restore the equilibrium of our souls, but which would have been ineffectual had we employed it at once.

B. *Proximate Preparation*

The proximate preparation consists of two things: to prepare the subject of the meditation and to be more recollected some moments before the beginning of mental prayer. To prepare the subject of the meditation is to choose a subject adapted to the end we propose to ourselves and to foresee the use we will make of it to attain that end.

If we could hope that God alone would act in meditation we should not need to prepare a subject, for the Spirit of God would supply it to us. This sometimes happens to faithful souls; but it is an eminent favor which God does not pledge Himself to give us and upon which we cannot therefore reckon. Now, the preparation for mental prayer consists not only in the dispositions of the mind and the heart, but also in choosing the subject, a matter upon which the faculties of our soul and God Himself are to act.

However varied the subjects of mental prayer may be, they may all be classed under three heads, according to the three states in which souls may be that want to go to God: the state of beginners, of those that are entering the purgative, and of those that are in the illuminative way.

For beginners: some truths of faith concerning the greatness of Jesus Christ; some also concerning the prerogatives of Mary. At times it may be very profitable to select as subjects the Last Things of man or the Passion of our Lord.

Those entering upon the purgative way and wishing to make a general review of their conscience, those that need to excite themselves to deep sentiments of repentance, that feel the necessity of appeasing the justice of God and of drawing down His mercy, will take for their meditation all the subjects that will make them understand better what it is to offend God and to profane the

Blood of Jesus Christ: they may also take all those that may incite them to confidence in the divine mercy.

Those who are walking in the illuminative way ought to choose ordinarily the mysteries of our Lord Jesus Christ or of His august Mother. Therein they will learn how to tell the different virtues which they should practice and which will excite and inspire them to a higher degree of justice in view of these two great Models.

Anticipating those who think that they cannot find suitable matter for preparation and therefore excuse themselves from any effort in this regard, Father Chaminade indignantly asks:

How is that possible? Without going farther, are you so ignorant that you do not recall a few words from your catechism or the principal mysteries of your faith. Recall that God sent His Son to you, that the divine Savior became incarnate, that He lived and died for you? How is it possible that these truths make no impression for you? Is it impossible for you at least to think of them, to examine them, to consider them, or to retrace them before your eyes? Is not this something to interest you? Here it is a matter of your redemption, of your predestination!

C. *Immediate Preparation*

There are three things to do upon entry into mental prayer: (a) place ourselves in the presence of God by an act of faith, believing firmly that He is everywhere, that He is in the place where we are, and that He is in our hearts. Thus we are obliged to adore Him and to maintain ourselves with respect before His divine Majesty; (b) recognize ourselves as unworthy to appear before Him because of our sins, ask His pardon by an act of contrition, and unite ourselves to our Lord Jesus Christ, to appear before His Father and to pray in His name; (c) and realize that of ourselves we are incapable of making mental prayer in a way useful for our salvation and beseech the assistance of the Holy Spirit to make it well.

It is very easy to place oneself in the presence of God. Since God is present everywhere, wherever we might be, it is true to say that we are in His presence at all times and in all places. It is only that we do not think of this, we do not take cognizance of it. It suffices, then, to place ourselves in God's presence at the beginning of mental prayer by recalling that God, who sees us and hears us, is truly there and by paying attention to this truth.

It is not at all necessary to represent God to oneself under a sensory image; there is nothing like God. Let us not depart from this truth; God is simple and unique. We cannot define Him; yet where is the man, thinking upon Him in silence and recollection, who cannot find Him in his heart and know Him there?

If we are before the Blessed Sacrament, although it can be done also elsewhere, it is good to represent the adorable Person of our Lord Jesus Christ to ourselves under the form which we can imagine He had while on earth. We shall there recognize God, and we shall adore Him in our Lord Jesus Christ. There is no more agreeable or more glorious homage for God.

God is immense, hence He is everywhere, hence He sees all, hence He is here, hence I am under His eyes. God is the Creator who made me according to the idea He had of me from all eternity; there is nothing in me that God did not put there. On other occasions you can reason in the same way upon God the Conserver of all things.

I am before the God of heaven and earth, before God strong and awesome, before that immense, infinite Being who created all things with a word, who set the laws of the entire universe, and who presides over their observance! His hand supports the earth. The sun and the moon know His voice. All nature proclaims His grandeur, His magnificence, and His adorable perfections. I am before the Avenger of vice and the Rewarder of virtue. I am before Him who will be my Judge; His eyes light up the very depths of my heart; my most secret thoughts are known to Him. Who knows but that He has His hand upraised to punish me? Who am I, then, to dare appear before Him? Who am I to lay claim to these most intimate communications with His Sacred Heart?

O Lord, penetrate my soul with the thought of Your divine presence, my mind with the notion of Your infinite perfections, my heart with Your unspeakable lovableness! Penetrate me with the fear of Your judgments, with the most intense sorrow for my past disorders and my present infidelities! Increase in me the light of faith that, knowing You better and knowing myself better, I may no longer love anything but You, I may no longer think of anything but You, I may no longer see anything but You! It is for these ends that I am at Your feet to consider, by the light of faith which streams from Your adorable countenance, the truths of faith. Help me, save me for I can do nothing without You!

How long shall I continue these acts as the introduction to my meditation someone will ask. I say, first of all, that one cannot assign any determined time. I say, in the second place, that one ought to remain with the introduction as long as the Spirit of God draws the soul on. In the third place, that such a person who remains quite long on these acts is really making mental prayer if he spends his entire time in this holy exercise; for he will attain its end. Finally, I add that it is necessary that the heart, the sentiments and conviction of faith produce these different acts in the exercise of the presence of God and not a habit wholly natural and mechanical.

To the presence of God the children of Mary will join the presence of their Mother. From the heights of heaven she has fixed her eyes upon her children. She is always disposed to aid them in their prayers as in their combats. Let us never lose sight of this sweet thought; it is as true as it is consoling.

If, as I have the happiness to believe, Mary is our necessary and universal Mediatrix, I conclude that it is impossible to make mental prayer without Mary. If no one knows the Father but the Son and those to whom the Son has revealed Him, equally no one knows the Son but His Mother and the Church to whom she has revealed Him. Let us unite ourselves, then to Mary in mental prayer! And let us beseech her who knew Him so well and who studied Him so well to make her Son known to us. She has gathered together and has preserved so religiously in her heart all the words which came from His lips!

O divine Mary, Mother of my Savior Jesus Christ, my Mediatrix and my Advocate with Him, O my tender Mother, my confidence in the mediation of your Son is troubled at the sight of His holiness and my own unworthiness. I have recourse to you. I shall give myself to Him. I shall always turn my glance toward you. Jesus Christ will always be kindly toward me if I am with you and if you are with me. You are all my hope!

Let all your meditations be referred to God through Jesus Christ, with Him, and in Him. Such is the universal practice of rendering to God the glory which we owe Him, of obtaining all the grace which we need, and of acquiring the holiness to which we are called. This practice is very easy if we remain habitually with the Blessed Virgin.

In preparing our meditation let us not, therefore, pass on without examining the part she bore in it. For instance, is it not incontestable that, at the very moment that the Blessed Virgin saw the executioners preparing for the crucifixion of her adorable Son, she offered Him to God, not only as being the Son of God, but also as being her own Son, and because, as Mother, she possessed genuine rights and a real authority over Him? It would be right and proper to make this the first point of the meditation. In all our meditations, a loving union with Mary is always to be presupposed. A meditation made without Mary is indeed a very poor meditation.

An excellent means to make a good meditation is often to elevate one's heart to Mary. In a meditation on the mysteries of Jesus Christ consider the part that Mary bore in them; in a meditation on moral truths, consider the perfect, the excelling practice of it in the life of the divine Mary.

Consider that the Son of God in His humanity looks down from heaven upon all the people of the world, but especially upon Christians, who are His children, and more especially yet upon those who are actually at prayer and in whom He sees the good or bad use they are making of it. Imagine that Jesus Christ is in the same place as you, as though you see Him before you, in much the same way as you represent your friends.

D. Body of the Meditation

The body of mental prayer includes three points. The first consists in considering our Lord, Jesus Christ, in relation to the subject of meditation and in rendering Him homage. The second consists in three things: (a) convincing oneself that what was considered in the first point is of great importance, (b) applying it to oneself, (c) asking it of God with fervor. The third point consists in taking firm resolutions.

If the best made mental prayer were that wherein the soul has developed beautiful thoughts and exact considerations, we would have to conclude that contemplation is not so perfect; for there the soul does nothing but behold, like a child who considers without seeking the why and the wherefor. Such a conclusion is evidently contrary to the principles of prayer.

The soul in the presence of God does not hold forth on some topic. It does not permit itself long discourses or reasonings. It listens to the Holy Spirit, and it beseeches Him to speak when He seems to be keeping quiet. Enlightened by faith, supported by hope, and embraced by charity, it rises to God without forcing itself and without effort.

The considerations, therefore, ought to be made: (a) without effort — without doing too great violence to our imagination; (b) with simplicity — not reasoning too much; (c) with faith — supporting our reasoning by the Gospel; (d) with devotion — serving ourselves from time to time with holy aspirations and fervent expressions.

The first thing in beginning the meditation is to cast your eyes upon our Lord and consider, with a serious attention and a profound respect, His actions, His words, and His sentiments touching on the subject of the meditation. Next, render to Jesus Christ the due which St. Augustine recommends: adoration, admiration, praise, love, thanks, congratulations, or compassion (if the subject is a sorrowful mystery). This method is very exact; for we ought to be images of Jesus Christ — His actions ought to be the models for our own. Then convince yourself of the importance of the subject on which you are meditating by weighing the reasons for it and by sounding out its motive. Afterward apply the subject to yourself; understand well the need you have of this truth or virtue, note the faults you have committed and find out their source. Be truly sorry that you are so little in conformity with ardor, confidence, humility, and perseverance.

The considerations are made in various manners but always in view of the end proposed in the meditation. First, examine in the light of faith the general sense of the words which express the truth being meditated upon. Second, examine the particular sense of several expressions. Third, when there is question of truths or fact, take them up as a narration of the details which enter into them. Fourth, this is especially useful for beginners, consider the impression produced by the subject on each of the senses and faculties and powers of the soul.

If the considerations have been well made, especially if they have been made in the presence of God, they will produce their effect upon the heart. Thus, one will feel himself more or less moved, more or less touched by some sentiment of love or fear or compassion according to the subject meditated upon.

Each one must apply the subject to himself, i.e., he must: (a) understand the need he has to fill himself with the truth or virtue upon which he is meditating; (b) note the faults which he has committed in this matter and uncover their sources; (c) conceive sorrow and confusion for being so little conformed to Jesus Christ in this regard; (d) ask this conformity with ardor, confidence, humility, and perseverance. To be heard in his pleas, he should have recourse to the merits of Jesus Christ, to the intercession of the Blessed Virgin, of St. Joseph, of the holy angels, and of his patron saints.

When there is question of taking resolutions which are more difficult or more painful to nature and to self-love, you must represent to yourself the strength and the courage which our Lord brought out in His great resolutions taken and carried out for the glory of His Father. Jesus Christ determined to spend His entire life in the service of His Father, to pass it in abjection and suffering, and even to give it up on the ignominy of the cross. Nothing could turn Him from His resolve; fearsomeness did not shake His constancy. And although He suffered all that the most cruel fury of men and the rage of demons could devise against Him, He never put off the execution of what He had resolved to do.

It is an illusion to make general resolutions; one forgets them so soon! Thus, if someone were to ask you halfway through the day what resolution you have taken, you would have to reply, "Ah, I do not remember." Ask the Spirit of God to make you understand what resolutions you should take. Let us not have the humiliation of having taken resolutions and of having forgotten them.

To form resolutions, one must apply to himself, to his own conduct, the truths he has just meditated upon. He must see wherein he is still lacking in their regard. Such is called "the reflection upon oneself." This act is made by way of examen which one insists upon more or less according to personal need.

E. Conclusion of the Meditation

Let us sigh in sorrow for having opened our heart so little to the Holy Spirit and having so little responded to the movements of His grace when He incited us to produce holy affections. Let us confound ourselves for having had so little respect for so high a Majesty. Let us ask pardon for our distractions, light-mindedness, and for all the other faults which we have committed.

Choose some thought to which the principal considerations and affections are attached; this thought is known as the "spiritual bouquet" which could be the truth of faith which you have been meditating upon. You should renew it by frequent acts throughout the day.

We ought to gather together some of the good thoughts and holy affections which God gave us during mental prayer to make of them a spiritual bouquet, which by its fragrance and presence, might renew in us from time to time during the day the good sentiments which we have had in this holy exercise, thereby re-creating us, so to say, and strengthening us in our trials and labors.

An exercise of such importance as mental prayer is worth the while to follow it up. It has not been so carefully prepared in order afterward to abandon the results to hazard. The fruit of mental prayer depends not only upon the care devoted to its proper performance, but also on the recollection which follows it immediately.

Remember that the intervals between your meditations are, or ought to be, only the continuation of mental prayer. Are you occupied with crucifying the old man in you? You must continue this work, and this continuation may be called also the continuation of mental prayer. Our whole life then ought to be a continuation of mental prayer — a life of prayer.

IV. DIFFICULTIES IN MEDITATION

I would ask those persons who complain of their dryness and distractions the following questions. How do you make mental prayer? What zeal, what good will do you bring to it? What efforts do you make to repel the distractions which besiege you? What is the nature of these distractions? Do they come from the mind or from the heart? How, respectively, do you repulse them? What are, in fine, the causes of all this dryness, of all these distractions?

Mental prayer is not to be an exercise of penance or of patience. We must go to it with good will, with our heart full of faith. Sometimes God makes us bear trials; but these are not ordinarily of long duration, especially in the beginning. When disgust lasts too long, the spiritual director is to see whether the subject is making all his other prayers well. It is commonly one's own fault when mental prayer becomes so difficult.

We can have great illusions concerning prayer. Provided it be made, whether well or badly, we do not push our examination further. Among those who perform their prayer in such a manner are some who say, "I am not wearied by prayer. I do not find it long." I can well believe that; they pass all their time in distractions, which do nothing more than amuse them.

It is not surprising to find some who complain of being tormented by an infinity of distractions in their prayers and of not having the slightest taste for meditation. No wonder! They perform their duties entirely in a human way and still think that their actions have great merit with God. If they would enter into their heart, they would without doubt see that they are carrying out their duties in a way unworthy of persons consecrated to God and that their distractions come from the continual dissipation which reigns in all their conduct.

Alas! they do not examine into these details. They even console themselves with the thought that their distractions are not voluntary; they go even so far as to believe that these distractions ought to be of great merit for them before God, because, as they say, such distractions are the occasions of struggle for them. God, who sees their conduct, judges differently in the matter. These souls will be greatly surprised on the last day when they behold themselves destitute of all merits in the eyes of the Lord, they who had considered themselves so rich in virtue and in merit before Him, being similar, in this respect, to the bishop of whom St. John the Apostle speaks in the Apocalypse. He performed all kinds of good works; he conceived the idea that these good works must render him very agreeable to the eyes of the Lord, and that he was thus amassing great riches in heaven. While he was engaged in these troubles God told him, through (the intermediary of) St. John, that he was greatly mistaken in his pride, since he was, in fact, very poor; that his actions were good in themselves, but performed in an altogether human manner, and that good works thus performed have no merit with Him. Our life is a life of meditation and of union with God; our life and our meditations should react upon each other, so that our life influences meditation, and meditation, our life.

Do not disquiet yourself over the numerous distractions in your prayers and even over an occasional vagary of your mind during work. The first rule to follow is to be patient. The second is to seek out the cause and destroy it. You will arrive at that, I hope, through the practice of interior recollection, learning thus to walk in the presence of God and to believe in His love.

Distractions may come from three sources, according as they are distractions of the passions, of levity, of trial or chastisement.

First source. Every distraction, which has for principle any ill-regulated affection whatever, is a distraction of the passions. A person may have passions capable of causing such effects. There is no other remedy than to combat, subdue, sacrifice, and root out the passions themselves that give rise to these distractions. The best means at our disposal would be meditation.

Second source. We often consider as a natural and excusable levity, the love of levity, which is, in reality, a passion. We can recognize by two signs whether the levity is natural and excusable. If the distractions have no fixed object. If they present themselves at any time: "Whatever proceeds from nature is always the same." But even then we can employ various devices either to vanquish it in part or at least to prevent its most deplorable effects.

Third source. Four things are to be considered. In what this state of trial and aridity or distraction during meditation consists, and in how far it is real. How we can recognize whether it is a state of trial and not a punishment from God, or an effect of justice on the part of an alienated and angered God? Two signs can be observed. If we are already virtuous when this takes place and if it does not hinder us from daily becoming more virtuous. Sometimes God permits those who lead the best lives to fall into this state. The manner in which we must conduct ourselves in order to render this state useful and salutary to ourselves is of vital importance. There are, therefore, rules to be used: To humiliate ourselves; to be docile in all things to the commands of God; to suffer without agitation and bitterness and, still more, without discouragement and despair; to be very careful not to abandon meditation or neglect it (example of Jesus in His agony); not to change anything in our practice of virtue, etc.

Do not be disturbed by distractions which try you during your mental prayer. As long as they are not voluntary and are not born of the heart, you have only to let them slip away from you as soon as you perceive them. The Blessed Virgin and our Lord, to whom you should unite yourself ever more closely, will supply for your frailty and lack of stableness of soul.

You are being tried by many distractions in your prayer. As long as they do not come from the heart, pay no attention to them. Turn away from them as soon as you notice them. Then humble yourself before God on their account, continue to pray as though you had not been interrupted by such distractions.

Many persons need to fix their imagination in order to be less distracted. That can easily be done with the representation of places, circumstances, persons, and the like. But one must be very temperate in these representations in proportion that the dispositions of faith, humility, and union with Christ and Mary increase. The imagination is far less troubled, and we need less to concern ourselves with it in meditations on historical events. There the imagination finds its natural habitat.

When you are not able easily to rid yourself of distractions, have recourse to meditational reading in which you will be able more easily to guard yourself against their actual importunity, though resolving to combat their cause outside of mental prayer.

I frequently experience in my mental prayer (says the imaginary soul) such a dryness and disgust that I can suffer it no longer. This dryness and disgust affects even my intellectual faculties and sometimes goes so far as to make me think that I have been rejected by God. I feel an extreme sadness and an inconceivable languor.

Dryness and disgust can come from a lack of preparation for mental prayer or, what is the same thing, from a lack of the proper dispositions for it. To enter into mental prayer without preparation, without the proper dispositions of soul, is, according to Scripture, to tempt God. God has made such great promises for prayer only on condition that the soul praying has the required dispositions or does all it can to clothe itself in suitable preparations.

Dryness coming from God is more rare than is thought. Often we attribute to God things which are more displeasing to Him than to the soul itself. It is for a wise spiritual director to discern when it is a trial from God. After he has examined seriously the ensemble of the life, efforts, and sentiments of the soul avowing such dryness, it is difficult for him to be mistaken when everything bears the seal of divine action.

One meets confessors who, on the avowal of their penitents, think they recognize that it would be better for them to give themselves to something other than mental prayer, since they make little or no progress in it. And with that in mind, they prescribe other practices of piety, such as spiritual reading and vocal prayers. What an illusion! Instead of looking for the cause of the evil to cut short its results, they say one should renounce so indispensable an exercise for every soul that would walk in the ways of perfection! What a decision! And how it reassures the penitent who asked for it! No more mental prayer until God comes back! In other words, remain far from God as long as God holds himself aloof.

One who makes so clear-cut a decision undoubtedly must not know that a St. Teresa was faithful for more than ten years to a prayer that was torture for her and that during so terrible an affliction she multiplied her meditations and visits to the Blessed Sacrament, although they were a martyrdom for her. St. Teresa would doubtless applaud such a decision. A St. John of the Cross was abandoned for years at a time by God, yet he was no less faithful to mental prayer. A St. Francis de Sales, a St. Ignatius were similarly tried; but in their times of desertion, they did not counsel themselves to withdraw from mental prayer. On the contrary, they applied themselves to it all the more. It is enough to open the lives of the saints to realize that they all acted that way.

In substantiation of this opinion, here are some detailed reasons that should convince a soul to remain with mental prayer:

a) Because disgust and wandering take their source in our lukewarmness and disloyalty.

b) Because disgust comes from the little use we make of prayer. It is only the usage of prayer that can dispel the disgust and distractions. Sweetness and consolations in prayer are the fruit and the recompense for a long life of prayer and not of individual and unconnected prayers.

c) Because our distress is frequently only a trial by which God wishes to purify us; hence, we must persevere in it.

d) Because we ought to view our troubles as the just punishment for our past infidelities.

e) Because God wishes sometimes to make this exile and this separation from Him in which we live more detestable than ever.

f) Because sometimes we are more inspired with conpunction for our past offenses in sensing the opposition and the revulsion they have left for truth and justice.

g) Because we must be purified still more of all that is too human in our piety.

Let us begin by drawing near to our God, and He will draw near imperceptibly to us. Let us fulfill the duties of our state. Let us watch over our senses and especially over our tongue. Let us live for God, live for heaven, live conformably to our sublime destiny.

After that, if our Lord still wants to try us, let us recognize and adore His sovereign goodness, let us recognize and acknowledge in all humility that we are useless servants.

It happens sometimes that God withdraws Himself, refuses sensible favors to certain souls, and, on the contrary, permits painful and obstinate temptation to torment them without a moment's rest. But such souls, in the very midst of their anguish often so cruel, never cease to have trust and to repose themselves upon the goodness and tenderness of the best of Fathers. Thus, despite their sufferings, they nonetheless have a source of peace to console them.

If you take care to conduct yourself as you ought in this state, you will profit greatly from it. Oh, my dear son, how happy is the soul when it can show to its God, by its fidelity to Him in the most terrible abandonment, that it is seeking Him alone! Possess your God in faith, for He is within you; and rejoice in this precious treasure, although it be hidden from your eyes. Go to Mary and ask her to show herself your Mother in showing you her Son. Only, my dear son, watch out not to give in to disgust; the demon would applaud at that, to the shame of heaven and your faith.

The soul experiences such great pains only because God means to inspire it with greater love for Himself. The more it submits, the more it kisses the paternal hand that chastises it, the more it is purified and the more it loves. For then it is the more loved, since mutual love tends toward greater strength and more intimate union. How precious then is faith, how meritorious, how it advances the work of purification!

Temptations, dryness in mental prayer, involuntary distractions, even sleep, also involuntary, in no way will do harm to your meditations and especially to their efficacy if you always remain united to our Lord, Jesus Christ. It is He who prays for you and who is your prayer. Do not desire consolations of that sensory fervor which is so delightful. Our Lord sees without doubt that you would become proud from it if you experienced it. Be faithful to Him without deviation and remain in peace.

CHAPTER THREE

Spirit of Faith and Presence of God

Our destiny is perfect union with God in heaven. We are to regain as much of that union as our fallen nature will permit us here on earth. On this earth the highest degree of union is expressed by the consummate virtues of the spirit of faith and in a continuous state of the presence of God. Everyone is in agreement that the spirit of faith and the presence of God can be best obtained, if not the only way, through well-performed daily meditation. For this reason Father Chaminade was so insistent on the practice and method of meditation. Many spiritual directors cannot lead their subjects beyond the formalities of meditation, and hence never more than mention the unitive stage of a soul on its way to God. But Father Chaminade felt sure that there are sufficient number of souls who attain the unitive way and thus must know what to expect in that state. We cannot aim for what we do not at least understand to a certain degree. This chapter, therefore, is a consideration of the fruit of daily persevering meditation and the closest union with God and the Blessed Virgin on earth, short of personal revelations.

I. WHAT IS FAITH?

Faith is the conviction we have of a truth. The light of faith is the motive which produces this conviction. The light of human faith is reason, the word of man; hence, its uncertainties and all its imperfections. The light of divine faith, of the faith of God is the Word of God Himself; it is the eternal production of His entire being; it is His Son; it is Jesus Christ inasmuch as He is God. Therefore, Jesus Christ is called the Word, the Word of God.

When, then, the light of faith penetrates our soul, it is the Word

120

of God who comes to dwell therein. This is not simply imagination. The Apostle, that is, the Holy Spirit in the mouth of the Apostle St. Paul, has revealed it to us: "Christ dwelling through faith in your hearts."

We do not see Jesus Christ in our soul when the light of faith enters. It is, in fact, not as man, such as He is in the Holy Eucharist, that He dwells therein, but as the Word of God. But if we do not see Him there, we feel all the qualities that He attributes to Himself. "I am," says our Lord, "the way, and the truth, and the life." In fact, by the light of faith and the faith which it produces in us, we come to know the truth of God; it animates us, it is our life; it shows us what we must do, the road we must follow.

If the light of faith is the Word of God; if because of it the adorable Word comes to live within us; then we understand that faith, the conviction resulting from this light, is precisely the union of Jesus Christ with us, a union which goes so far as to transform us in Jesus Christ. By faith, in fact, as we have seen, our enlightened mind no longer thinks but as Jesus Christ thinks. It is Jesus Christ who unites Himself to our heart; by faith our guided will no longer acts but, as Jesus Christ acts, it is Jesus Christ who united Himself to our will. Thus the new man is formed within us.

Faith affords us a large participation in the divine wisdom; hope, an assurance of beatitude produced by the Holy Spirit; charity, the love of God which inflames the heart. These three can be reduced to one, namely to that loving wisdom which enlightens the mind, reassures the memory, and fills the heart with holy delights. All of these goods are included in the possession of Jesus Christ.

Our Lord dwells in us other than by Holy Communion. It is not I who tell you this but St. Paul with these words, "May Jesus Christ dwell by faith in your heart." Jesus Christ dwells in our souls, working there the divine life — which is all included under the name of faith.

Do not be led to believe that if I attribute such wonderful effects to faith, I exclude the reception of the Holy Eucharist. On the contrary, it is by communion with Jesus Christ as Victim immolated on the cross that all these miraculous changes take place in Christian souls. But it is always faith which enables us to nourish ourselves with the sacred flesh and precious blood of Jesus Christ; it is by faith that our life becomes the life of Jesus Christ.

When the substantial union ceases in him who had communicated, faith maintains a moral union between his will and Christ's so intimate that it is not at all surprising that there should be reciprocal influences which constitute a very real spiritual communion.

Since our lamentable fall in the Garden of Eden, faith in Jesus Christ has been indispensably necessary for salvation so that whoever has not believed in Him has not been saved. But I would like to know what faith is intrinsically, faith in itself. Faith is that intimate adhesion of the soul to the promise which God made to Adam that His Son would become man to save the human race. For Adam had lost for himself and for his posterity eternal happiness and he merited by his sin of disobedience to the Creator all the terrible effects of His justice. The promise of a God is as immovably subsistent as God Himself. Therefore, to believe in Jesus Christ is to admit Jesus Christ into the soul because the promise of a God is a reality. He who has a complete confidence in it acts by it as being in himself. That is why the ancients were justified by their faith, Christians too are saved by their faith in the accomplishment of the promise.

Faith is the root of all virtues; it is from it that they draw the sap which makes them sprout and grow, as the root supplies the tree with the sap which gives it life. The more the roots spread themselves, the stronger the tree grows; so the greater our faith, the stronger our virtue becomes. Let us multiply our acts of faith during the day.

No doubt faith must be animated by charity. Faith should not only be a light in the mind but it should be in the heart as well. There must be in faith a disposition of the heart and love of truth. That is why you must savor what you believe. St. Paul tells us that it is the faith of the heart which justifies us.

True hope is that which is founded on faith, especially, says the Council of Trent on that article of it which states that the sinner is justified by the grace of the Savior; that is, that hope has for its object to become just, to become holy and virtuous, for that is what the word "justified" signifies.

To act by faith, to practice faith, and to live by faith, is to consider all things, natural or supernatural that happen to us, in the light in which God views them, and which we receive by faith, and then to judge them according to this light and to conform our life thereto.

Faith consists in seeing God in all things; to see Him in the person of superiors, in everyday occurrences, in the most ordinary actions of life. It is necessary, however, to give to this truth its whole extension; for revolutions, political changes, whatever occurs in general or happens to the individual, all come from God; not even a hair of our head falls without His permission. The death of a sparrow is surely no extraordinary occurrence, yet it happens not without the will of your heavenly Father. All comes from God. Suppose God should not permit a certain thing to happen, how could it come to pass? Nothing has strength or movement, or any quality unless from God! You may call them general laws; yet who sustains these general laws?

You believe that God is your all; you believe that He is your Creator. You believe that He is the preserver of your being; and you believe that He is your last end. Cherish these truths; cherish the truths which they essentially contain.

You believe that God is your all; you cherish this truth. Why not cherish the truth which it implies, namely, that you are nothing? Why, then, not love to annihilate yourself before His supreme majesty?

You believe that God is your Creator. Can you not love the Creator of your being? It is the love that He cherishes for you from all eternity, that prompted Him to create you. And do you not see in this faith in a God Creator, your absolute dependence on Him, and the need you therefore have of His providence, both in the order of nature and of grace? Cherish this dependence.

You believe that God is the preserver of your being; in Him you live and have your being. What sweet repose you ought to find in Him! Still, what childlike apprehension should not this position inspire, that God can destroy you at any moment, if you should displease Him!

You believe that God is your last end; that He created you only for Himself; and that only in Him can you find supreme and eternal happiness that your heart desires. Love the design of your Creator in your creation, as well as in the preservation of your being; but at the same time, love the duties which this blessed destiny entails; all your thoughts, all your actions, and all the concerns of your life must be referred to the last end of your creation.

In vain would the soul be enlightened by the most brilliant light of faith if the heart does not become pure; such faith, bound captive, would only make the soul more culpable and miserable. Hence all our efforts, all our labors, all our struggles must tend to purify our hearts, and this is truly the end and aim of Christianity. For to have a pure heart is to flee from sin and from the shadow of sin; to love only God, to seek only Him and tend only toward Him with all our strength; to observe His law, to fear His justice, to adore His supreme will; in a word, to have a pure heart is to practice faith, to pour into practice the lessons of faith; from which it follows that the faith which can see God is verily only that faith which purifies the heart, in other words, operative faith.

It is the will that must subject the understanding to the service of Jesus Christ, that must subject it to the yoke of faith, and that forbids us to withdraw its assent for the lack of evidence. For it is said: "For with the heart we believe unto justice. O foolish and slow of heart to believe" (Rom. 10:10).

Faith must be animated by charity. Faith must exist as a light not only in the mind, but must also be present in the heart. It must be that disposition of the heart which is faith itself and the love of truth; you must relish what you believe. That is why St. Paul tells us that it is faith of the heart which justifies. It is impossible to be justified except by this faith of the heart. It is this faith of the heart which imparts to me the divine fire; I approach this sacred fire, and gradually my heart is warmed to make either acts of love or acts of generous resolve.

I believe that, as the times become more evil, we must give ourselves more to mental prayer, and grow more and more in the spirit of faith. Therefore, let us strive to raise ourselves to the faith of Abraham and to believe against all hope. Besides, we work really only when we work for God. May His holy will be done.

As faith has directed and sustained in us our sanctification, it will guide and strengthen us in our apostolic mission. We are managing God's works; let us manage them with God through faith, divesting ourselves of all earthly and, especially, of all selfish views.

This life of faith ought to animate all our actions. In it may be found the remedy against every spiritual evil. It will help us to bear up with various contradictions, and aid us to support the daily trials and mortifications. It will further help us to work with ardor and perseverance at the correction of our faults, and will be a support and guide in mental prayer; it will lead us back from our distracted thoughts when we ought to be conversing with God about our spiritual needs; it will make us bring to the reception of the sacraments that fervor and diligence of preparation necessary to reap the fruits worthy of them.

You will remedy all your interior difficulties if the faith which is solidly established in your spirit passes entirely into your heart. We must love what we believe. We have powerful motives for credibility and we must, so to say, be only reasonable to submit our reason to faith. This submission is already a great favor of God. But it only precedes the submission of the heart and the heart is submissive only in loving. It is in this manner at least that I see it and it seems to me dangerous if we fail to see our faith in practice. Faith, this faith of the heart especially, is a great gift of God. It is for this purpose that we must always say, "Lord, increase our faith!" God accords this grace easily, so to say, when we exercise ourselves in the works of faith. Justice lives by faith. Oh my dear son, what happiness for us if we are able to walk the rest of our days in the beautiful ways of faith, act only by faith, live only by faith. The faith which illumines only our spirit will not give us the life of justice which is a divine life.

I consult what my faith says on the matter. I then compare it with my conduct. I see how weak and imperfect this faith is by the conduct I have demonstrated. I have only to humble myself, make acts of faith and ask the good Lord that He increase my faith. Then I adore Jesus Christ under the point of view which has touched me. I ask pardon for having known Him so poorly until now. Finally I listen to what my faith prescribes for the future in regard to this mystery and I ask from the goodness of Christ and His holy Mother the grace to be faithful.

You say quite audibly, "Faith and confidence work miracles." But I will hardly whisper it. Faith and confidence work miracles only as they are necessary, and only when we have exhausted the means which faith suggests. You do not think that you are permitted to count on miracles? There is no doubt, that in ordinary actions of our lives, we must not and do not reckon on miracles; that were tempting God. When, however, we are engaged in a work which is in the ordinary course of His providence, and comes under ordinary actions of our life, it is surely permitted, when obstacles rise in our way, to count on that special protection of God, which to us seems quite miraculous. We may thus count on this protection, when what we do is commanded by those invested with the proper authority.

What admirable faith was that of the august Mary. She believed in the mysteries which are announced to her and these mysteries are accomplished in her. They are accomplished only because she has believed. Faith, accomplishment. What a lesson for us. The same mysteries are announced to us. They will be accomplished if we have faith. They will be accomplished so to say in proportion to our faith.

Faith and, above all, living faith, is the great gift of God; that is why we have great need of repeating continually, "Lord, increase our faith."

I cannot help admiring, since some time, though alas too short a time, that Mary, in the moment of the Incarnation, was associated in the fecundity of the Eternal Father by her lively faith and was animated by an inconceivable charity, and thus engendered that sacred humanity with which her divine Son clothed Himself. My dear son, it is by faith also that we conceive Christ within ourselves. By faith Christ dwells in our hearts. All the gifts of the Divinity to Mary may be reduced to the faith which animated her, and which became in her the plenitude of grace, the fountain-head of life. As Mary, by faith, conceived Christ in the natural order, so we, by faith, may conceive Him in the spiritual order.

II. FAITH AND PRAYER

What we have said of mental prayer, that its purpose is to unite us with God until we are transformed into Him; what we have now said of faith, that its effect is to unite us with God until we are transformed into Him, shows the relationship that exists between prayer and faith. Faith is the means by which we attain the end of prayer.

Our soul, created in the image of God, was disfigured by the sin of Adam. It can become more and more like to God through mental prayer; for therein the faculties of the soul receive a light which is Truth and Love of Holiness for which God alone is the source. When we make mental prayer of faith, our understanding breaks away from darkness and is enlightened with divine brilliance. Consequently, it becomes seeing, and an illumined spirit like unto God. God is charity. God is all love and love of holiness. In good mental prayer of faith our will receives the warmth of this love. It becomes pure, holy, disengaged from all imperfection, thus becoming a likeness of the will of God, which loves the good alone and wills the holy alone. In making mental prayer of faith, we are carried up to the very happiness of God Himself. Our memory is wholly occupied with the happiness such as the saints enjoy in the joyous bosom of God. Thus it shares already here below in the happiness of heaven.

Through mental prayer of faith, we go away from the miseries and evils which afflicted Adam after his fall and enter again into the pristine state in which man was created in a way that is most meritorious, beautiful, and admirable. We are raised above the earth; we break the chains that tie us to the things of the world. By means of the considerations, affections, and resolutions, we fly as with wings to God Himself to communicate with Him, to hear His voice, to unite ourselves to Him, and to become like unto Him. Thus our soul becomes deified.

Therefore, faith is the means by which we attain the end of mental prayer. Unless you believe, you will not understand. Thus our text shows us that it is even the necessary means, for we consider union with God in mental prayer as knowledge and love.

Considered under its basic aspect, prayer is essentially founded on faith. Its object and its instrument should be that of faith. Carried on the wings of faith, the soul flies so to say to the very bosom of God.

In mental prayer the soul offers to God the greatest of sacrifice, that of its reason by faith. The soul attains to the knowledge of God and of itself, a double knowledge which leads it on to love and praise God as He demands. Mental prayer must depend altogether on faith, turn upon the truths of faith, and be made in the light of faith. Of itself the soul is incapable of mental prayer. The soul must abandon itself to the guidance of the Spirit of God in order to consider only that which He inspires it and as much as He inspires it, thus sacrificing its own intelligence to follow only the divine attractions.

We should not seek other knowledge through our considerations in mental prayer than that which faith gives us. We should not excite our will except by the motives suggested by faith. We ought not reject the light which the Holy Spirit would communicate to our understanding through the gifts of understanding, wisdom, knowledge, and counsel or the impressions which He would make on our wills through the gifts of fortitude, piety, and fear of the Lord. But of ourselves, we should hold to faith.

After having contemplated the great objects of faith, God and His law in mental prayer, the soul seeks to render an account of its faith. And almost right away, struck to see its faith so frail and unsteady, it exerts itself with fervor to ask God with the Apostles, "Lord, increase our faith," or with the centurion, "I believe Lord, but make up for what is lacking in my faith."

Since God delights in giving His grace during prayer, we must profit by these sweet moments to ask for help in all our supernatural and temporal needs; we ought especially to ask for a lively faith, for it is faith which raises us to the throne of God. All virtues are, indeed, very useful, especially to religious; but we find none that are more useful than faith. With this virtue there is no room for illusion of self-love; for everything passes between God and the soul, whereas, in the case of other virtues, there unhappily creeps in a spirit of self-love which robs it of all merit.

Since we go to mental prayer with the intention of preparing our spiritual arms to attack our invisible enemies and defend ourselves against their insults, it is there that we must learn how to use the weapons of faith; for there are no stronger ones to vanquish the spirits of darkness and repulse all the efforts of hell.

Mental prayer ought to be made according to the inspirations of faith, with the confidence of hope and the devotedness of charity. It is by these three conditions that earthly man is finally changed by mental prayer into a man of God and a faithful image of Jesus Christ.

III. AN ANALYSIS OF THE PRAYER OF FAITH

We often speak of an increase of faith, and it is a great grace which we ought to request of our Lord frequently. This increase can be taken as a greater vivacity of faith or a greater extension of it. Generally, we can believe that faith increases in extent when it goes from the implicit to the explicit. By implicit is meant "enveloped," whereas explicit means "developed." In meditating upon a truth, we perceive other truths contained in it; thus our faith in that truth becomes more explicit. And it becomes more and more explicit in proportion as we come back upon it to consider it with a great attention illumined by that interest which faith inspires. We thereby discover in it more (latent) truths than it has words.

In mental prayer of faith we learn the most beautiful things most quickly. It is time well employed, for instance, to plumb the depths of the mystery of the Most Holy Trinity. Therein we can consider the unity of God and the distinction of Persons. Meanwhile, faith keeps us from extravagance. This mystery of the Most Holy Trinity, having been well meditated upon, looked into according to its length and breadth and depth, casts a marvelous light upon all the other mysteries of Jesus Christ. Moreover, we must always ask ourselves what faith has to say to us. Persons versed in contemplation and advanced in perfection see a great number of truths in the light of faith, a chain of truths which ravishes them and makes them love more and more what they see. Such is faith with love.

To exercise our faith, we must apply the elements of our faith to a revealed truth, make acts of faith of the heart and of the lips, draw out the consequences which flow from it and compare our conduct with them, deplore our blindness, humiliate ourselves, beg pardon of our Lord, ask Him for an increase of faith, and desire such an increase with ardor. Surely anyone who would do this will end by being heard in heaven; and little by little he will receive more vivid light. Through such an increase of faith, hope will become stronger and love will become more intense and pure, while humility will become more profound, regret more poignant, and desire to see God more ardent. In proportion as the soul is faithful, God will be pleased to enlighten it more. Such, then, are the delightful fruits of such an unspeakable communication of the soul with its God.

It is thus that the soul, in the mental prayer of faith, learns of God and of itself; these two kinds of knowledge are so joined together that to advance in one is to advance in the other. In contemplating the infinite perfection of the Divinity, the soul attaches itself to His love with greater fervor and thereby becomes capable of sacrifice. Its heart becomes pure, divine love sets up its empire within it, and the soul begins to experience anticipated delights of heaven.

Take the mystery of the Incarnation, for example. If we really believe that Jesus Christ is God, eternally begotten in the bosom of God, that He took upon Himself our nature, that by baptism we are incorporated in Jesus Christ — if we believe that, then we shall appreciate and respect our character as Christians, and we shall fear to do anything unworthy of a Christian.

We believe this truth; we make repeated acts of faith in it. We ask ourselves as Jesus Christ asked of the holy woman, "Dost thou believe this?" And we repeat it to ourselves until we can say with some truth, "Yes, I believe it!" We then apply it to ourselves and say, "If I believe that, what ought I do, what ought I think? That which I ought to think and do, do I do it now, think it now? Have I always believed this truth? Have I always acted in accord with it?" And we review our past faults. It is thus that faith awakens in us and penetrates us. It illumines our mind, warms our heart, and strengthens our will; and we are led to fervent sentiments and good resolutions.

Do you wish, for instance, to meditate upon heaven? Represent Jesus Christ asking you whether you believe there is a heaven, where for all eternity the saints will be flooded with a torrent of delights, and answer our Lord, "Yes, I believe!" If you believe that you have been created to enjoy this happiness, make acts of faith and think of the means you must take to arrive there.

Is this method which we have just exposed a true form of mental prayer? I reply, first, that all the Fathers of the spiritual life have recognized it to be a true form of mental prayer. The name by which they have designated it would prove this, for they have always called it mixed mental prayer. Second, the end and the great object of mental prayer is, assuredly, to purify one's heart and dispose one's soul to see God. Now, we see God here below only through faith. It is faith that makes Him known to us as He intends to be known. All the traits which He has made luminous before our eyes and which touch on His nature and marvels have been gathered together by the Apostles into one shining cluster of truth. This faith which makes God known to us is also a faith which justifies, which purifies the heart. Who, then, cannot understand that to contemplate the beautiful truths of faith in their ensemble is necessarily to make mental prayer? I should like to know what he is doing who, after having recited the Creed orally, recites it mentally pausing at each article as long as grace draws him on to exercise his faith. Is that not mental prayer?

When one prays the prayer of faith, his intellect rises out of its darkness. It is illumined with the divine light and becomes a spirit seeing as God sees, illumined as God is. The will receives the ardor of His love; it becomes pure, holy, free of imperfections, and similar to the will of God which loves only good and wishes only what is holy. The memory becomes occupied with the happiness of the saints, and it participates already here on earth in the beatitude of heaven.

IV. THE APOSTLES' CREED AND MENTAL PRAYER

Everyone should have a sufficient instruction in the Creed which is proportionate to the dispositions of his mind. Those who can learn only the lessons of the catechism will set themselves to master them; those who can do more should read a great deal on this subject. A true will and a real devotedness must also be supposed. There is no hope for anyone who does not will to make mental prayer.

Our practice is for the mind at the same time that it is for the heart; our mental prayer is simultaneously discursive and affective. Its manner of disposing the considerations is so true and its subjects of thought are so multiple that the mind passes from one to the other, so the heart is touched or not, without giving in to the enemy in the least. Thus, if you can only recite the Creed, content yourself with recitation. If you can meditate, do that. In any case, you are exercising yourself in faith; for you are formulating acts of faith with the heart and the mouth. Your time is thus spent among many acts, diverse by nature and suitable in their variety to fix your attention better.

After placing himself in the presence of God, as we shall explain later, the subject will recite first of all the entire Creed with all the attention of which he is capable. Then he will repeat mentally this recitation, article by article, considering each article until he no longer feels any taste for it in order not to open the door to distractions. If some articles do not make an impression on his heart, he should not stop with them because there should be neither effort nor contention in his prayer. If the beginner is disposed in such a manner interiorly that he is able to pause only a minute on each article of faith without being distracted, then he should stop just a minute. If it is even less, then he should pause less than a minute. But he must take care to be always attentive, letting the distractions pass in his spirit like clouds carried by the wind. He should be content to recite the Creed two, three, or four times if it is necessary, provided he does it with all the attention possible.

No matter how much progress the beginner has made in mental prayer, no matter how much good will he shows, he should not excuse himself from reciting the Apostles' Creed in its entirety first of all. This is intended to exercise his faith upon the whole magnificent ensemble of truths. Then only should he exercise himself upon the principal articles one after another.

One should not overplay himself too much in the beginning; for the aim proposed is principally to cut short any distraction. Thus, he should stop only a few instants at each article and even forbid himself a pause at those which do not appeal to him. Otherwise, reason becomes bored and the will disgusted.

It is only when a person has reached a point of attentiveness where he can spend the whole time of mental prayer in a state of relative calm that he should let himself stop longer at an article. It always holds good for everyone, however, not to stay with those articles which have lost their taste or which touch the heart only slightly but solely with those which move him. It is likewise worthwhile that everyone return during the course of the day to those thoughts which struck him during mental prayer, thereby to exercise his faith more on those points.

It is of principle that soon the soul will not find time enough to go over each article of the Creed if it has used its mental prayer with all the fidelity of which it is capable according to the manner recommended. Certain articles in particular will strike the soul more than others. On these a person should stop longer and come back upon them during the day as often as possible to repeat acts of faith, hope, and charity.

The manner which should be followed for the reflections on each article is easy. I take, for example, the second article of the Creed. I recite it mentally with all the attention possible. Then I hold myself in silence, listening to the spirit of God. If I feel some interior attraction to contemplate Jesus Christ as Savior, or as Son of God, as King, Priest, Pontiff, or Redeemer, I stop to consider Him under the point of view which appeals to me. I interrogate my faith and I compare it with my conduct.

At another time I consider the mystery of the Son of God become man. I behold either the wisdom or the power or the good-

ness of God in this mystery. The abasement of the Son who does
not fear to take on the form of a slave and the greatness of the
wrong done to this Man par excellence for our healing, I might
next consider. One by one I look into all the wonders of this
mystery; thus God conceived by a divine operation in the womb
of a Virgin, a Virgin conceiving without ceasing to be a virgin, a
God hidden under the weak covering of a body carried in the womb
of a woman.

I exercise my faith on all these marvels. Then I seek out the
consequences which follow from them for my heart and personal
conduct. Humility, appreciation, love are so many necessary out-
comes of my faith in this great mystery. And from these consequences, as from principles, other practical truths flow forth which
I also behold in the light of faith and of which I beg God and His
Son to grant me the happy possession.

It might be thought that a beginner would quickly fatigue himself in returning always on the same truths, always on the Creed.
This is a folly! If we faithfully follow this method indicated, we
would soon see that the contrary is true. It might also be thought
that we can never arrive at the making of a half hour of prayer
without distractions. Another folly! It is an illusion just as harmful
as the first.

Who does not see that all prayer which does not have faith for
object, for means, and for principle is a false prayer? And I ask
what that person does who, after reciting orally the Creed, recites
it mentally and stops on each article as long as grace attracts him
in order to exercise his faith, if he does not make a true prayer.

I desire that you see in this little sketch, the general practice
of the life of faith in the ordinary course of life, and especially in
mental prayer, which is the pivot upon which turns the whole
Christian and religious life.

V. PRESENCE OF GOD

When faith has gained a strong foothold in the soul, it loves
to consider itself in the presence of God as well as in that of the
sacred humanity of Christ.

Mental prayer of the presence of God, united to mental prayer of faith, is the peaceful contemplation of the presence of God, in which the soul, looking upon Him in the light of faith, gives Him all the attention of its heart and will. Ceaselessly in the light of faith the soul beholds Him and does not desist in its contemplation of His attributes and their effects.

What is the outcome? The bond uniting the soul to God becomes closer; there is a more intimate communication, and God diffuses Himself as it were, in the soul that prays. When faith has made considerable headway in a soul it loves to dwell in the thought of the presence of God and of the sacred humanity of Christ. Faith binds us in a way with God; it brings us into communication with God, merges our spirit with His Spirit, our heart with His Heart. The light of His Spirit passes into ours, we see things only as God sees them; we judge them as God Himself judges them; gradually our prejudices are scattered, we become adept in the science of God Himself, and this is the science of the saints.

All that God is is everywhere; otherwise He would have parts and would be divisible. But God can only be most simple and, consequently, indivisible. It is true, nonetheless, that He is infinitely great and that no place can contain Him. Yet He has no more beauty and goodness, no more liberty and power in heaven and in all the world than in the smallest grain of sand and in the tiniest drop of water. There is as much presence and power in one as in the other.

The three Persons of the Holy Trinity dwell in man: God the Father who created us, God the Son who redeemed us, God the Holy Spirit who sanctified us. Oh, what a consoling thought for man to have within himself the Holy Trinity! Yes, it is the most certain truth that God is within us and acts with us.

This presence of God in the souls of the just consists noticeably in His operation. He does not cease working the effects of His grace in them, differently, however, according to the dispositions which each one brings with it. Thus, in some His operation is strong, continuous, and sensible, whereas in others it is slow, weak, often interrupted, and reduced to only slight results.

It is essential to accustom oneself to the presence of God, but to the presence of God in a view of faith. God sees me! Who is this God who sees me? A just God who weighs all my words and who understands them all. A good God who wants only to reward me, who is always ready to come to my aid when I call upon Him. I say to myself sometimes, after I have pursued some vagary of my passions, "How could I have forgotten that God is present?"

Who can ever commit sin when he recalls that God is present, when he says to himself, "God sees me. God is looking down upon me." Not only does the sinner commit his crime in the presence of God, but he does it within God Himself, for His infinite majesty fills all things. He thus in a sense makes God Himself a servant of his iniquity.

Let us surrender ourselves solely and entirely to the guidance of the Spirit of God who dwells within us, manifesting thereby our persuasion that He will use us infinitely better than we can use ourselves! With such assurance, let us try ever to be in a state of pure emptiness concerning our own plans, desires, sentiments, and movements. Let us remain in a state of simplicity, and naked dependence of God, of passivity regarding Him, of indifference to everything, and of readiness for anything, of expectancy toward His movement in the execution of His designs and works in which we take only the part He wishes for us!

We must avoid, we must remove whatever obstacles to the presence of God which lie in our way, such as wandering of the mind, foolishness, and dissipation; we must exercise ourselves in the five silences of the preparatory state. As long as we occupy ourselves with creatures, how can we expect to think of God and hear Him speak? God must be present in our soul as our soul is present in God. Let all that we do be worthy of this Divinity!

This sentiment should generally prevail in all our actions, to retain us within the bounds of duty, to keep us from saying or doing anything unreasonable, and to excite us to good works, rousing us from time to time by the thoughts so familiar to the holy Prophet, "As the Lord liveth, before whose face I stand." We should entertain this sentiment especially in the spiritual exercises, in order to avoid negligence, irreverence, the wandering of our thoughts, and many other faults which we are guilty of in our devotions. All these indicate a lack of faith which lack renders them not only useless, but even harmful.

From the moment we awake until we fall asleep again, during work as well as during the necessary recreations, the religious soul must without effort keep up the idea of God's presence. All souls are led to this by wise and prudent spiritual directors.

Attention may be be given to the work in hand, but the intention must always be directed toward God; much the same as a person cannot help feeling the heat of the sun when exposed to its rays.

It is by making such acts that we place ourselves in the presence of God. All these acts must turn on the two fundamental truths: God is all, and I am nothing. Make acts of faith in these two truths, and listen to the inspirations of the Spirit of God in regard to these truths, behold the whole of the exercise of the presence of God.

We become accustomed to the presence of God little by little through our attention and fidelity to Him. We must make frequent acts of faith until His presence becomes continual. Such is a special gift which we must ask of Him and for which we must make ourselves worthy. That will demand sacrifices.

There are various manners of being in the presence of God, two of which are active and involve the soul's effort and two are passive and come as rewards directly from God. The first manner occurs when we actually place ourselves in God's presence. The second occurs when we have acquired the habit of walking in His presence. The third occurs when God Himself works in the soul; for this reason it is called passive. Ordinarily, however, such operation lasts but a short time, for a quarter of an hour at most, unless God deigns to give the gift of His presence. Such a gift, which is the fourth manner, is very rare.

Upon rising we must raise our mind and heart to God, under whose eyes we have passed the night, and prepare ourselves thus for mental prayer as we promptly and modestly dress. Throughout the day we must make frequent aspirations which will raise our soul to heaven with their ardent desires. In all our actions we must accustom ourselves to purify our intentions, to see God alone, to see Him in our neighbor and particularly in our superiors and confessor. In this way, little by little, faith will determine, accompany, and regulate all our actions.

Once the habit of the presence of God has been acquired, with what facility will the soul place itself before Him! There will be no longer any need of effort or constraint; for the presence of God, habitual in thought and affection, will imprint vivacity and unspeakable sweetness on the acts of the soul and its faith.

This continual exercise of the presence of God preserves our purity of soul in a most admirable way, sanctifies our ordinary actions, and brings us to undertake extraordinary ones for God, makes us profit from all occasions to practice virtue, and draws us insensibly to a high perfection. We cannot apply ourselves to it too much. We must do so, however, in a mild, easy, and free manner in which the heart has more of a part than the head.

To make this application to God more continual, the soul should keep itself in a simple view of God, accompanied by a loving inclination of the heart. From time to time it should strengthen its affective view with reflections on God's adorable perfections. Such a simple regard of the mind and sweet ardor of the heart, such an aspiration and transport of the heart sustained by a regard of the mind should be made without a multiplicity of acts or, at least, a great frequency of them. The soul remains fixed and strongly attached to its divine Object as far as human fragility permits.

VI.   PRESENCE OF GOD IN MENTAL PRAYER

I observe that those who wish to advance seriously in mental prayer exercise themselves frequently with the thought of the presence of God outside of the time prescribed for mental prayer. In this manner by the habit they acquire, they need less time to renew themselves in the presence of God at the beginning of their meditation.

Those who, outside of the exercises of piety and particularly of mental prayer, do not have the habit of the presence of God experience great difficulty in placing themselves and in keeping themselves in His presence during mental prayer and holy Mass. Such is the great cause of the little success they attain in the ways of perfection. The reason why so few persons succeed in mental prayer is that so few acquire this holy habit of the presence of God. Ask any number of people how they spend their days, how they make their various exercises of piety, and you will learn that they have not grown familiar with the idea that God is with them. They frequently forget it even during their prayers. After that, should we be astonished not to see them succeed in mental prayer? For myself, I affirm that I would be more astonished to see them succeed. It is useless to dwell longer on the necessity of growing accustomed to the thought of the presence of God; that necessity is too evident by itself to require more ample demonstration.

When someone has an intense desire to speak with God, he finds no greater happiness than when the moment arrives for mental prayer. For then he is able to speak to God and open his heart to Him completely. Even though he has been in converse with God during the course of the day, he does not judge that enough, since he did not tell Him all that he wishes to tell Him in mental prayer.

We must begin mental prayer with an act of faith in the presence of God and in His immensity before whom we are a mere nothing of body and soul; a nothing of essence, of faculty, and of action; a nothing of every good, whether of nature or of grace.

Faith in the presence of God is supremely great as it is present everywhere, present and working especially in us, in the natural as well as in the supernatural order. Acts of adoration and above all of confusion, of humiliation, and of contrition, these should be prolonged for some moments.

The soul, in the presence of God, wholly penetrated by His greatness and excellence and by its own abjection and profound misery, bows itself down to earth in self-renouncement and adoration. It invokes the aid of the Holy Spirit and of the august Mary, then it surrenders itself to Their enlightened guidance. It takes care not to follow its own lights, for it realizes their vanity, feebleness, and insufficiency. If it considers, if it examines, it does so because the Holy Spirit is gently urging it thus. It has only to open its eyes to the light of faith, and immediately it sees, it admires, it contemplates, and it considers itself most happy to see and to contemplate. It praises God and it thanks Him. It deplores its ingratitude and it implores His pardon. It does not enter into lengthy reasoning; but it hearkens to the Holy Spirit and begs Him to speak to it when He appears to be silent. Enlightened by faith, supported by hope, and inflamed with divine love, it raises itself to God without commotion or effort, once again it does not discuss matters.

After these preparations have been made, you will hold yourself in the presence of God in the greatest recollection. The disposition of your soul during this recollection is that of a simple sentiment of faith, of hope, of charity, or of resignation to the will of God. Let aside all the ideas, reasoning, and sentiment which your imagination might suggest in order to be guided by that holy simplicity which I have always recommended to you.

We are not rejecting the method of mental prayer which we have traced, but we must not confuse mental prayer itself with its method. It is wise, in making mental prayer of faith and of the presence of God, to use the means which the method suggests the better to consider the truths which faith uncovers for us or to guide our affections, as well as to fix our resolutions. But we must do this always with prudence and discretion.

To make mental prayer, it is not necessary, as perhaps we think, that we must have the actual thought of the presence of God. We know only too well that the ever actual thought of the presence of God is a favor from heaven which is as rare as it is precious and which God gives only to a few privileged souls. What is being asked of us is the habitual thought of the presence of God, that is, the happy faculty of holding ourselves in His presence. This habit is acquired by frequent repetition of acts.

I would say, first of all, that no determined time should be assigned to making acts of the presence of God in mental prayer. In the second place, we should rest in this holy presence just as long as the Holy Spirit attracts us. In the third place, I would say that we have really made mental prayer even if we pass all the time in this holy exercise because we have done all that is required for mental prayer and have attained its end. Finally, I would add that it should be the heart, the sentiment, the conviction of faith which produces the various acts of the exercise of the presence of God and not a natural habit that is completely mechanical.

It requires a sort of intrepidity at the beginning in order to maintain the practice of the presence of God in meditation. On the one hand we must banish the thought of every creature and of every interest in it or affection for it; we must withdraw from ourselves; we must divest ourselves, so to speak, of self-love. On the other hand we little know the infinite amiability of God toward whom we wish to tend as to our last end. We must, therefore, not be surprised at any feeling of disgust or at any number of distractions. Nevertheless we should have recourse to various contrivances to keep up our good will and to strengthen the feeling in the faith of God's presence, the memory may dwell upon texts relating to the same, and the imagination may help to represent oneself as immersed in God.

Where then could we seek God if the light of faith did not reveal Him to us as before us and within ourselves? Let us not forget that the means to make our meditations well and profitably is never to begin them without being deeply penetrated with the presence of God and having made several acts of lively faith in this adorable presence. For, if we really feel that God sees us, hears us, and hears the most hidden secrets of our hearts, how could it come to pass that we would not reap any fruit from the inestimable favor of conversing with God!

CHAPTER FOUR

The Interior Life

Father Chaminade frequently spoke and wrote on the topic of the interior life, a subject closely allied to that of the spirit of faith and presence of God. If the result of mental prayer is the life of faith and the presence of God, then, in turn, the result of these two is the interior life. For that reason we have devoted the next chapter to a consideration of the interior life and the spirit of that life — the Spirit of Christ.

Conformity with the state and mysteries of Jesus Christ while on earth is the only means of obtaining a true interior spirit. We have already explained the meaning of the mysteries of Christ and the spirit of Christ in Chapter Two of Part One. It is this spirit we must make operative in our souls that we might facilitate the inflowing of the true interior life and spirit.

To live is to have an interior principle of movement. To live spiritually is to have no other interior principle of movement than the Holy Spirit, to act only by Spirit of Jesus Christ, to live only His spirit, and to cease all other movements. To live according to the flesh is to have as interior principle of one's thoughts and actions the inspirations of the flesh or of corrupted nature.

St. Paul felt within himself two men, as it were, one of which wished only good, the other only evil. It is the same in us. Why? It is because there are in us two principles of life, one of the spiritual life and the other of sin, of concupiscence. As Christians it is the Holy Spirit who is our principle of life and who awakens in us the desire for virtue. But there is also concupiscence, the principal evil, which leads us to sin. Hence the battle. What the Spirit wishes, the flesh does not, and vice versa. As a result the Spirit must fight against the flesh, otherwise we shall die.

Can it be said that he who does not give in to his passions and vices, who commits no great sins, who mortifies himself even in certain things, lives a spiritual life? No. The spiritual life is the very life of Jesus Christ. St. Paul expresses it, "It is now no longer I that live, but Christ lives in me" (Gal. 2:20). A true religious is another Jesus Christ. A true Christian is also another Jesus Christ.

That which is called LIFE is an interior principle of movement. It is the Holy Spirit who dwells in us. The Spirit of God enlightens us just as He did Jesus Christ. St. Paul says, "Have this mind in you which was also in Christ Jesus" (Phil. 2:5). If you live the life of Christ you will see as He does, think, feel, love, and judge as He does.

In this properly consists the Christian life, that the Christian live interiorly by the operation of the Spirit in the manner that Jesus Christ lived. Without that there is no unity, no perfect conformity to the Ideal to which our Savior calls us and which He wishes us to live with Him by the operation of the Spirit. It is to be a life veritably one with the Father and the Son living only one life, one sentiment, one desire, one love, one light because they are only one God in two Persons.

Behold why the Apostle calls the Christian man, the spiritual, interior man; whereas, he calls the worldly-minded man and the sinner, the exterior man. He wishes to teach us that, as soon as our soul has received the Spirit of God, and is really animated with this Spirit, our whole life becomes almost invisible and interior. Our most ordinary actions are then sanctified by the sacred faith that purifies them; the Holy Spirit regulates our desires, reforms our judgments, renews our affections, spiritualizes our views; all that we see is perceived only through the eyes of faith; the whole world is nothing more than an open book, which unceasingly discloses to us the wonderful works of God and the prodigious blindness and folly of the majority of men.

The conformity with Jesus Christ that we ought to have is that which we should have with His interior mysteries. Thus our souls should become conformed in their sentiments and dispositions not only to the exterior mysteries of Christ but also to the interior states that our Lord had in these same mysteries.

Or again, this conformity consists in resembling Christ in His exterior mysteries which are as the sacraments of the interior mysteries that should be operated in souls. Thus as our Savior has been crucified exteriorly, it is necessary that we be crucified interiorly. As He has been buried exteriorly, it is necessary that we be buried interiorly. This interior life that is expressed by the exterior mysteries and the graces acquired by these same mysteries ought to be in all, since they have been merited for all.

The spirit of these holy mysteries is given us by baptism and it operates in us the graces and the sentiments which have relation and conformity to the mysteries of Jesus Christ. Follow Christ, imitate His actions, go to Him, go after Him; you will never stray in following in His footsteps. The dignity and the merit of His Person invites us to follow Him, and it is for us an honor of infinite value to be similar to Him by a living expression of the life that He led when He was among men.

Therefore, the essential is the interior, and we must be most earnestly occupied with it. As regards the rest, we shall receive whatever it may please God to bestow upon us. The spirit of Jesus Christ is a spirit of retirement, of recollection, and of prayer. It is also a spirit of renunciation and of penance and, lastly, it is a spirit of fortitude.

How can we maintain the interior life in the midst of daily business? It is precisely then that the interior life is most indispensable, and we must be penetrated with it to such an extent as to carry it with us wherever we go, even into the midst of the most distracting surroundings.

As to the reasons which you allege regarding the needs of your own sanctification, namely, the indispensable necessity of the retreat, I have but to remark that you must learn to preserve the spirit of retirement, of solitude, and of recollection, amid the affairs with which you are occupied, as well in your travels, as in the visits which you are obliged to make. Be on your guard, lest your numerous occupations prove detrimental to the interior spirit. The greater the amount of work or the number of occupations, and the bulk of business of every kind, the greater also the need of prudence, of patience, of meditation, and of recollection. May the activity of your mind, and the very ardor with which you serve your neighbor, not stifle within you the interior operation of grace. May it not interrupt that constant abandonment of yourself into the hands of God, as a victim, which you should offer to him without ceasing. A certain moderation in the practice of charity is often productive of more good than is accomplished by following its energetic activity. If you desire to advance in the ways of God, you must be entirely submissive to His grace and totally dependent upon the operation of His Holy Spirit.

Accustom yourself to watch over your heart. Direct all its movements toward God alone, and toward His holy service, not by an intense application of your mind, but through love. Your natural activity may prove harmful to this interior life, which impels us to seek God in all things, and to seek Him alone.

Whom shall we choose as our patron and model in acquiring this interior spirit? It is the august Mother of God, whose life was spent for God alone and who constantly carried God about with her with perfect submission to His divine will.

Mary herself was the first one to be conceived of Jesus Christ according to the Spirit of Jesus Christ was Himself conceived according to nature in her virginal womb. Mary was formed interiorly to the resemblance of Jesus, her adorable Son, and associated from then on in all His mysteries, in order that the conformity might be as perfect as possible, or rather that there might be uniformity possible.

To serve God as Mary did is, in other words, taking into account our limited ability, to serve Him as did Jesus; for, in shaping Mary, grace took Jesus for model, and this august Virgin is so perfect and so pleasing to God only in consequence of her most exact resemblance to Him who is the eternal delight of the Most High. Thus is the imitation of Mary the surest, shortest, and easiest way of imitating Jesus Christ.

The imitation of Jesus, through resemblance to Mary, is therefore essential. Now, the life of Mary as a copy of that of Jesus, displays three distinguishing traits. The threefold object: (a) cease-lessly to strive for our own sanctification; (b) to labor at the salvation of others; (c) incessantly to be on our guard lest we be contaminated by our necessary preoccupation with world-minded affairs.

An eternal love unites the three divine Persons. This same love which He receives from His Father, Jesus Christ relays to us, for He loves us, as He Himself says, as His Father loves Him. "As the Father loved me, I also have loved you." The love He demands of us is the same.

Are you living members of Jesus Christ, animated by His Spirit? In a word, do you love God? No, it isn't possible. No, my Brothers, indolence, coldness, and negligence toward the things of heaven are not compatible with the love of God. Is it love when we are indifferent about being distant from Him, without a desire to be united to Him, to fear the moment that calls us to Him? Alas, we have not even begun to love!

Charity subsists with faith and hope. In fact, it cannot subsist without them, for it does not yet enjoy the divine object which it loves and which it does not yet see face to face. It can only contemplate it with the eyes of faith and it needs hope which gives it the wings to fly to it as to the unique end and supreme happiness of man. But aided by the breath of the Holy Spirit and enflamed with His ardor, it lifts itself above itself and loses itself in the bosom of the Father, there to love Him, even though it sees Him only by the eyes of faith, with the same love as the saints who contemplate Him clearly such as He is, with the same love which the divine Persons have for one another.

Let us strive earnestly to obtain the pure love of God, and a profound contempt of self, and then the Holy Spirit will lead us on to the accomplishment of great things. When shall we be so truly stripped of self as to love God only in Himself and for Himself? Do we love Him with a pure love by loving Him with selfish interest? Does not self-love tarnish the pure love of God?

My beloved is unto me and I am unto Him. This is the maxim of the saints in heaven, and here on earth our motto should be the same. We must belong entirely to God just as the saints belong entirely to Him, to think only of Him, to love Him alone, to live for Him only. How unfortunate should we be, were it otherwise, since Providence has been so lavish of Its graces that we might live as saints upon earth. God has placed us in the very laboratory of heaven, there to practice what we are to do eternally; namely, to love God and to love Him alone. Could we ask the dwellers of the heavenly realms what they do in heaven, we should receive this answer: "We love God." Is He alone the source and object of your eternal bliss? And we should again be told: "Yes, God is the sole object of all our happiness." We should be able truthfully to give the same replies.

What ought our sentiments to be when we behold the works of God and remember that all has been made for us! What gratitude and what love should fill our hearts toward a God, who, for the happiness of His creatures, has done so much over and above the necessary! The sun has been made to give us light — might He not have made it less brilliant? Might not the firmament which fills with admiration those who contemplate it, have been decked with less splendor and magnificence? The earth might have been made to bring forth merely the necessary sustenance without furnishing such a diversity of good products that delight our taste. But what is all this compared with the gift God makes of Himself, and how ought not His thoughtfulness spur us on to love God and seek Him alone!

Yes undoubtedly, God loves us, and we shall never be able to state how great this love is, for all that we could say would be as nothing compared with that love. Now if God loves us with a generous, unvarying, persevering love, that recoils before no obstacle, and finds no sacrifice too great, it is with this love that the saints have loved Him, and that we ought to love Him, if with the saints we wish to partake of the glory that Jesus Christ has merited for us. Besides, could we do too much for a God who has done so much for us? "And ought it not suffice," says St. Augustine, "that God simply allowed us to love Him, that our hearts would dilate with the greatest love for Him?"

At times, in moments of great fervor, we beg God to take this heart, to leave it no longer in our hands, and to let no one take possession of it. Would God take this heart by force? Never, He has given man his will, and He will have man give himself freely. The sun has been created to give light; it must follow its orbit and cannot do otherwise; the same may be affirmed of all creatures subject to man. But our heart is free, if we sincerely desire it. God alone will be the object of our love, and we shall exclaim with the Spouse of the Sacred Canticle: "I love my beloved, I have chosen him among a thousand." Let us perform all our actions only to please Him, and let us beware lest any human motive mar the purity of our love.

CHAPTER FIVE

Self-Abnegation

Last, but not least, one of the means of conquering the "old man" and controlling the five silences in our quest for perfection, is self-abnegation, or mortification. Self-abnegation is an essential aid for all men in every topic that Father Chaminade has developed in this book. Without self-abnegation, which includes all the forms of imposing control on the fallen nature of man, we would become weak, irresolute, and succumb to all the wishes of the flesh, the world, and the devil.

The character of the perfect Christian is to be dead to the world as Jesus Christ was and with Jesus Christ; the destiny of the perfect Christian is to rise like Jesus Christ and with Jesus Christ.

Two great oracles: death and life. The vices and the passions give death. To battle them is to seek life. It is therefore death or life, heaven or hell, to live according to the flesh or to live according to the Spirit.

The Savior of the world came as a victim; He lived a life of privations, He died overwhelmed with sorrow; and the sword of sorrow likewise pierced the heart of His divine Mother. No better lot could befall the disciple than that of resembling his Master. If Jesus Christ requires of His disciples to die to the world, it is to vivify them with His own life, and to transform them into Himself.

Understand that the old man has been crucified in Jesus Christ in order that the body of sin be destroyed and we commit it no more. In order to properly understand this text, we must know: (a) That in every sacrifice we can distinguish an interior one and an exterior one. The exterior one is the sensible victim that is im-

molated and destroyed; and the interior one is the oblation of self
to God by which one recognizes the sovereign domain of God over
all creatures. (b) That by the old man is meant depraved nature,
passion, concupiscence, and the inclination to evil. Now the death
of Jesus Christ properly signifies our old man. Such is the interpretation of the phrase: The death of Christ signifies the destruction of
our other nature. With the above explanation, this text is easily
understood. The exterior sacrifice of Jesus Christ is our old man
and this old man, which is the body of sin has been sacrificed at
the same time as Jesus Christ, that is, at the same time that Jesus
Christ is immolated internally with the old man. Jesus has immolated this old man in order that the body of sin be destroyed,
that is, that concupiscence and our inclination to evil be conquered
by the grace which He has merited and which does not allow us
to sin again.

The exterior and bloody sacrifice is not the only one of which
Jesus Christ is our model on Calvary. The interior sacrifice of submission, of obedience to His Father's will, has never been interrupted. The character of the perpetual sacrifice of Jesus Christ is
His perfect submission to the divine will. The first act of this sacrifice was to say to His Father on entering the world, "I come to do
your will." The continuation of this sacrifice during His life was,
as He Himself said, in doing whatever the Father willed. The
consummation of this sacrifice was to say to God in accepting the
chalice of His Passion, "Father, not my will but thine be done,"
and to be obedient unto His death on the cross. The perpetuity
of this sacrifice in heaven is to have but one will with His Father
and on earth to reunite all men to Himself, if possible, in the
perfect submission which is due the Sovereign Majesty of God.
The sacrifice that He demands of His creatures, then, ought to be
an interior one, as is His in the divine Eucharist. It ought to be
more a sacrifice of their soul than their body, more the sacrifice of
their natural inclinations and their earthly desires than their temporal goods, more the sacrifice of their will always submissive to the
Will divine, always in complete conformity with the will of the
Father as was Jesus Christ's.

Exteriorly he ought to be like the victim of the Old Law, and interiorly like the victim of our salvation under the sacramental species. The former were bound to the altar, made senseless, butchered, and burned in the holocaustal fire. This is the model of our sacrifice as to the exterior. The latter, without giving any sign of life, is nevertheless living the life of God. This is our model as to the interior.

It is not merely this death that Jesus Christ demands of His disciples. If He desires them to die to the world, it is to make them partakers of His life, and to transform them into other Christs. He must feel within himself only Jesus, and what Jesus has felt.

This death is unto life. If we divest ourselves of the old man, it is to put on the new; if we renounce the creature, it is in order to attach ourselves to the Creator; if we are void of self, it is in order to be filled with God; if we attain to hating ourselves, it is in order to love God all the more. This constitutes the purpose and end of self-abnegation.

Let us seek God only, by a complete self-abnegation; this should be our motto, which is contained in these words, "Abnegation in spirit."

The generous soul, after having renounced all to follow Jesus Christ, will without difficulty accomplish this great precept which is the end of the law, as also the object of religious perfection. "Thou shall love the Lord thy God with thy whole heart, with thy whole soul, with thy whole mind and with thy whole strength."

We feel how universal is the self-denial required by so perfect a love, a self-denial that tears us from things terrestrial to bind us to God alone. These two advantages are inseparable and mutually sustain each other; absolute detachment leads to perfect charity, which consists in loving God.

With our whole heart — the heart, shorn of every earthly affection and self-love, will in the future turn wholly toward God.

With our whole mind — no more vain and frivolous thoughts.

With our whole soul — as long as life lasts and uninterruptedly.

With all our strength — all the faculties of our souls and bodies in the full intensity of their strength will be constantly directed toward God, furthering His glory.

The union divine, the transformation into God, the life by God and in God, the pure love of God — all are made the more perfect in direct proportion to our progress in self-denial, in the interior detachment from every creature, in the crucifixion, in the death and the burial of the old man.

Self-denial, as to the body, consists in not being solicitous about it, nor about the conveniences it demands. Too great a nicety regarding drink, food, and the daily requirements of life must be crucified. Small inconveniences are offered to God by acknowledging that they are but trivial.

Sickness, mortification, crosses, and sufferings of every nature detach us from the world and ourselves, and direct us to God. "I thank the Lord for having sent me this sickness," exclaimed an ill priest. "It has helped me to understand the nothingness of things; only what is eternal is truly great and worthy of appreciation. I have become quite a different man through this sickness sent by Almighty God." Withal, he had led a very regular life; yet trials purify the just man, and render him more holy.

God shows clearly the necessity of contradiction and trials by placing before us His divine Son crucified and telling us that Christ had thus to suffer in order to enter into His glory. If therefore we wish to enter into His glory by following the Spouse, we must, after His example, suffer and suffer valiantly and generously whatever may be pleasing to Him, without choice or condition on our part. If such be our motive, far from dreading sufferings we shall love them.

But if we have not as yet attained these generous dispositions, and if our nature revolts at the very thought of contradiction or suffering, what are we to do? Excite ourselves to patience, and consider the advantages of the cross. The contemplation of Jesus Christ in His sufferings and humility will teach us, more than all else, how to suffer and be humble and His unalterable patience will teach us patience.

Persistent patience is therefore the most salutary means we can use to bear up to the end under all oppositions to natural inclinations, and at the hour of death we shall rejoice at having been able thus to have merited the crown of life. The perfect compensation will be ours; and if, after all, we could have a regret, it would be not to have suffered more. Let this thought encourage us; let us not be vanquished by our weakness, but let us vanquish it. If labor inspires us with fear, then let the prospective reward lend us new vigor!

I do not favor for you extraordinary penances nor prolonged vigils; but, by way of compensation, I advise an interior and an exterior abnegation which ought to be the outcome of your mental prayer and the pains you take to be recollected.

Those who love and esteem mortification will sedulously seek the means of mortification, joyfully acquire its practices, and delight in them after the example of the saints.

We will then mortify our caprices and our inclinations, mortify all our passions in general, mortify every passion in particular, but, more especially, our predominant passion. We will mortify self-conceit in its manifestations. (a) Curiosity, which seeks novelty and delights in the study of things rare and extraordinary. (b) Pride, or vanity of the mind, which leads us to imagine ourselves above our station and urges us to pierce and scrutinize the secrets and the exalted majesty of divine Providence; or it impels us to aim at understanding what is incomprehensible in the divine mysteries, and induces us to pursue such studies as will attract the attention of the public. (c) Light-mindedness, which keeps our minds in a state of continual distraction, gives ready admittance to every passing thought, busies us with ever so many events and visionary projects and leads us to pass, without taking any special interest, from one thought to another, from one study and occupation to another, and thus robs us of all the fruits of our toil. (d) An excessive activity of the mind, which soon becomes involved in wild reasoning, is agitated, troubled, disquieted, grows impatient, and, in the end, but heats the brain and accomplishes nothing. (e) Stubbornness and obstinacy.

We must also mortify our own judgment, taking as our model Jesus Christ, passing as He did through all the stages of infancy. Our own judgment takes the liberty to examine inquisitively, and often to condemn, inconsiderately, the actions, the motives, and the conduct of others. It unscrupulously rejects the advice given by superiors, when this advice is contrary to our tastes; or, going still further before submitting, it must know all the reasons.

Lastly, we must mortify self-will.

If you would come to Jesus, the practice of these mortifications well understood will give you a fair start, will continue the work and crown it with success. But above all it must have these two qualities: it must be constant and universal.

Abnegation is the renouncement of self, and self-renouncement is the abdication of self-will. If ever any true joy can be experienced in the world, it is to be found in practice of perfect obedience. Half and half religious (or the Christians) are always disquieted, and how can they be content with themselves if God is not? On the other hand, what will our sentiments be at the hours of death, and who will then console us? Consolation will then come from the sacrifices brought to God, especially the practice of obedience.

Do you not know the true happiness on earth consists in doing the holy will of God? If you wish to carry your burden with ease, unite in spirit with our Savior Jesus Christ who will give you new courage and strength, and will render sweet and light what is now bitter and oppressive.

Say with me from your heart, "All glory and honor to God alone." As long as you live in yourself and of yourself, and not by the spirit of Jesus Christ, you may apply to yourself the reproach made by the prophet to the Jews, after the Babylonian captivity, "You have sown abundantly but your crop has been ruined." The true means of success is to divest yourself entirely of self and to abandon entirely to the Spirit of the Lord.

Why do you not consider every suffering and humiliation as divinized, not only in the person of our Lord Jesus Christ, but also in every one of His members? Why do you not taste the happiness of those who suffer, the happiness of those who are humiliated. You must make it your duty to be faithful to the utmost, and consequently, you must be severe toward yourself. Finally, you must heartily endeavor not to do your own sweet will, but that of God alone, of Jesus Christ. "Christ did not please himself" (Rom. 15:3).

Examine well how Jesus left this world, and the kind of death

He suffered. The spiritual life consists in living as Jesus, of Jesus, and in Jesus.

To believe that by punctually following a timetable we may lead a more spiritual life, if at the same time we are not ready to suffer all manner of contempt, humiliation, and persecution, is a great illusion. If we cannot do what Jesus has done — for never has man suffered or will he suffer as He or as much as He — we must at least love to live as He did, that is poor, destitute of everything, deprived even of necessities, to suffer because we cannot have new things at once, etc. If we do not experience these sentiments, we may be convinced that we have not the spirit of Jesus Christ but the spirit of the worldly-minded. If we fly from humiliations, it means to say that we have not the spirit of Jesus Christ. What a surprising contrast between our lives and that of Jesus Christ! What cause for confusion! The least reproach disconcerts us, we feel piqued over an apparently harsh word. If we are humbled, or seemingly despised and not accounted much, we lose the peace of our souls, we are troubled and manifest exteriorly our impatience and interior revolt. What a sad contrast between our lives and that of Jesus Christ.

As Christians we are all consecrated to the cross. The title "Christian" obliges us essentially, not only to carry, but even to embrace with joy, the cross of Christ. For to speak of a Christian is to speak of a being whose profession is to follow His Head, who is Jesus Christ, over His painful route of sufferings and humiliations. And it becomes for him not only a duty but an honor and a glory.

We are destined to be attached to the cross, owing to the condition of our birth. Children of a guilty father, we cannot expect to find happiness on this earth, where he, through his sin in Paradise, has incurred the wrath of God. And who is the man that can claim exemption from suffering? Even infants, newly born, announce by their cries that they feel the miseries of life. As they advance in age, the assaults of corrupt nature harass them continually. At times pride causes suffering because of their inability to outstrip their fellow men. Again ambition leads them to undergo multiplied fatigues to amass riches with which they may procure the sweets of life. And what next? They no sooner have attained the goal of their ardent desires, than, volatile enough, they turn to something else. All their efforts are abortive. No one can promise himself a life serene and cloudless, and even those who revel in wealth and honors are often the most unfortunate.

We have been consecrated to the cross through the grace of baptism. Several ceremonies of the sacrament of baptism bring home this truth. The crosses made upon our bodies with the holy oils, the water poured on our heads in the form of the cross, all remind us that the Christian is not only to carry but to embrace the cross of Jesus. For it speaks of a Christian, speaks of a man who professes to follow Christ in the thorny path of humiliation and suffering. To bear the cross with Jesus must be for the Christian not merely a duty but an honor and a glory.

By our vocation to be a Christian or to be a religious, we have been called to carry the cross. God, foreseeing that morals would eventually become corrupt in the world, wished in His infinite mercy to separate Christians from Christians. On this account He instituted the religious state, in which He commanded the religious to do what is only counseled by God in a special manner and in that way they are specially consecrated to the cross of Jesus.

What was the constant occupation of our Lord during His mortal career? He constantly sought the lost sheep, heedless of labor and humiliations, ardently desiring to shed His blood in order to save them. Never did His Apostles see Him so desirous to go to Jerusalem as on the day on which He was to be betrayed. Following His example, should we not spend ourselves entirely to help our neighbor, entertain that zeal, that ardor and desire of their salvation, which lead us to embrace cheerfully all the sufferings of our state, and even to go in search of the cross, in order to be crucified?

Besides, the more we cherish the cross, the less painful it becomes; while if we dread it, and carry it reluctantly, it will become all the more burdensome, and not much fruit will attend our labors. We shall never be truly happy until we lovingly embrace the cross, since it is for this reason that our divine Christ has chosen us.

It happens at times that God withdraws, that He refuses His sensible favors to certain souls, and that He permits, on the contrary, painful and obstinate temptations to torment them, leaving them not a moment's repose. But these souls, in the very midst of their anguish so severe at times, continue to have confidence and to trust in the goodness and tenderness of the best of fathers. But if we must suffer, let us consider the prize of sufferings and we shall feel new courage arising within us; let us embrace suffering with joy, and we shall render ourselves worthy of the glorious title of spouses of Jesus Christ.

If the demons unceasingly persecute the Church of Jesus Christ, how are they to be spared who join together in defending it, they especially who declare themselves children of Mary and who unite precisely to fight against the empire of Satan? Are we not strong with the strength that the first prophecy pronounced against the serpent gives to us: "I will put enmities between thee and the woman, and thy seed and her seed; she shall crush thy head and thou shalt lie in wait for her heel"?

Man leans upon God, and God supports him. God speaks and will have man believe and be well penetrated by His word. He pours out His sweetness and His grace into the soul, or He makes it see clearly its weakness, its misery, its sin. Then comes a holy fervor by which the soul must be set aglow and to which it must correspond by good resolutions. The soul hears God's voice and draws nigh to Him and is more closely united to Him in proportion as the heart corresponds to His divine communications.

Sometimes it seems as if God does not speak; the soul is subject to aridity and unavoidable distractions. However, if man labors earnestly in mental prayer, it is no proof that God is not with him and in his heart. It is rather that God wishes to test the fidelity of the soul that is conversing with Him. If man seeks only to please God, he will thereby acquire more merit and be less exposed to pride.

The greater our charity, the more our virtues and our affections will be purified; the soul becomes all love and all its desires are at the end; for it knows the object it loves, as itself is known and loved by it.

The incense of mental prayer sends forth its perfume only through the fire of mortifications. When someone cannot make mental prayer, he should examine whether he is a mortified person;

for, without mortification, mental prayer is impossible. If we cannot succeed in mental prayer, it is because we seek our ease, not wishing to suffer or to be deprived of anything.

To your temporal sufferings are added spiritual trials, and, behold, you are at the mercy of every variety of adverse circumstances. Oh! now surely you must raise the shield of faith; for this shield is impenetrable to any darts whatsoever. I imagine I see the courageous St. Teresa saying without interruption in a spirit of faith, "Yes, poverty is better than riches; it is the road to Heaven. The good Jesus has not where to lay His head. Humiliation is the gem of eternal glory, and fairest livery of the Christian. It was only through humiliation that Christ entered into glory, etc." Come on then, be courageous; especially as you have invincible arms. I am loath to part with you. May the Spirit of God animate you; you can have no courage excepting through Him.

You are weary, you say, of all those contradictions, and I admit that if you see them only in the light of reason, there are some that might discourage; but if you see them in the light of faith and in the order of Divine Providence, you will never waver, and your peace of soul will never alter. All the pains that we both experience will not, I hope, be lost before God. Since it is for Him and while doing His work that we experience these trials, let us only strive to preserve true patience according to faith.

You tell me, you would need the patience of an angel. I shall add that you need a divine patience. Christian patience is a participation in the patience of Jesus Christ. A general exercise helpful toward progress in the virtues of patience, mortification, and humility is to be united in a spirit of faith and love with the Sacred Heart of Jesus, suffering, mortified, and humbled. Let us not complain of the weight of our cross. The cross He willed to carry for us was incomparably heavier!

Why does Jesus Christ take the beautiful name of the Lamb? It is because, in reality, He has been immolated for us as a lamb to the justice of His Father. What should not be the sentiments of the soul toward the immolated Jesus if she wishes to be completely united to Him? Jesus who died for you and was immolated like a lamb, still lives, and nevertheless immolates Himself constantly. What a mystery of love! How can we be so indifferent! How cold are our hearts which pretend to be united with the most loving and most amiable Jesus.

Look up to Jesus to learn what qualities the victim must have, and how it must be offered. He is a victim and a victim of charity! He has offered Himself and constantly offers both Himself and us, provided we are united with His sacrifice of love. Jesus Christ so loves this state of a victim that its character remains with Him in His heavenly glory. It is thus He showed Himself to St. John, when He allowed the latter to see, in a vision, the happiness and privileges of virgins in heaven. When He ascended into heaven, on the day of His Ascension, He bore on His sacred body the five wounds which He had received on the cross. You understand well the meaning of all this. You must try to be still more faithful; you must be adorned with the virtues which most please Jesus — humility, charity, the spirit of sacrifice, filial confidence, purity. You must be penetrated with so ardent and generous a love as to be united to Him through self-immolation and self-sacrifice.

Let not the activity of your mind, or your ardent desire to help others, prevent the workings of grace within you, nor interrupt your filial trust in God, which places you as a victim in His hands. A certain moderation in the practice of charity often accomplishes more good than a display of too much activity.

Be bent on acting only through a spirit of humility and self-annihilation. If you have not, as yet, acquired these sentiments, your being offered to the Lord as a victim will profit you but little. God will have humble victims. If you wish to serve Him, be completely submissive to His grace, and dependent upon the inspiration of His Spirit.

You have now begun to realize the difficulty of carrying out in practice the offering you have made of yourself as a victim. Presumably you will observe that, the more you strive to carry out your noble purpose, the greater will be the repugnance you experience, for nature will ever struggle, as does the victim that is about to be immolated. But your faith, your love of the Lamb of God that was slain, the value of the humiliations which Jesus Christ has deified in His sacred Person, the justice of God, which must be appeased for you and for others — all these supernatural views, if they sink deep into your soul, will permit you to smile at difficulties, which seemed mountain-high.

Strengthen yourself in the practice of true virtue, especially in the spirit of mental prayer and of faith, and in self-denial. Sentiments of penance, mortification, humility, and recollection are particularly valuable. Be faithful to these; they will lead you on to good mental prayer, which in turn will increase these sentiments.

If you are mortified, especially with interior mortification, and if you are a man of mental prayer — and you can never be the one without the other — you will supply for all your deficiencies.

There remains only this to say — "Let the name of the children of Mary and saints of God be synonymous. May the Father and the Son and the Holy Spirit be glorified in all places through the Immaculate Virgin Mary. Amen."

Selected Bibliography

Armbruster, Jean-Baptiste, S.M., Editor, *Ecrits de Direction* (Fribourg, Switzerland: Marianist Seminary, 1954–1958), three volumes.

Burns, Norbert C., S.M., *Ascetical Formation at the Origin of the Society of Mary (Marianists)* (Rome: Angelicum, 1955).

Chaminade, William Joseph, *Our Knowledge of Mary* (Dayton: Marianist Publications, 1956).

Cole, William J., S.M., *The Spiritual Maternity of Mary According to the Writings of Father William Joseph Chaminade* (Mount St. John, Dayton, Ohio: Marianist Publications, 1959).

Elbert, John A., S.M., *Filial Piety, the Ideal Devotion to Mary* (Dayton: Marianist Publications, 1952), pamphlet.

―――― *Mental Prayer in the Marianist Way of Life* (Dayton: Marianist Publications, 1955), pamphlet.

Greiner, Francis J., S.M., *From a Full Heart: Thoughts from Father Chaminade* (St. Meinrad: Grail Publications, 1949), pamphlet.

―――― *The Spiritual Way of an Apostle of Mary* (St. Meinrad: Grail Publications).

Harrington, John, S.M., *The Teaching of William Joseph Chaminade, Founder of the Society of Mary (Marianists on Mental Prayer)* (Dayton: Marianist Publications, 1960).

Resch, Peter A., S.M., *The Marianist Year* (St. Meinrad: Grail Publications, 1946).

―――― *The Prayer Life of a Religious* (New York: Benziger, 1948).

Stanley, Thomas A., S.M., *The Mystical Body of Christ According to the Writings of Father William Joseph Chaminade* (Fribourg: St. Paul's Press, 1952; Dayton: Marianist Publications).

Index